THEN & NOW

SMITHTOWN

OPPOSITE: Marion Howell Deutzman (on tractor) and Lillian Medwig Maybee (working the backhoe) attend to the fields of James D. Maloney's Flowerfield Bulb Farm in 1942. Situated at the corner of Mills Pond and North Country Roads in St. James, the farm was in operation from 1909 until the middle part of the 20th century. For more information on Flowerfield, see page 39. (Courtesy Smithtown Historical Society.)

THEN & NOW

SMITHTOWN

Bradley Harris, Kiernan Lannon,

and Joshua Ruff

Photographs by John DiGiacomo

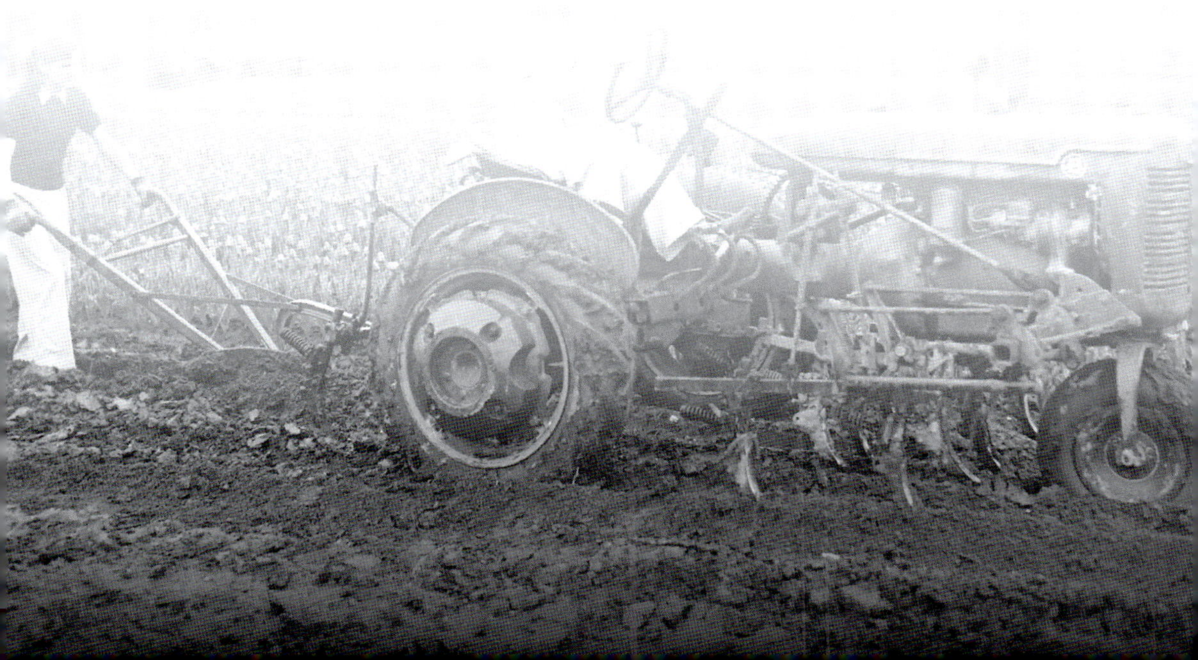

ISBN 978-0-7385-7514-8

Library of Congress Control Number: 2010940167

Published by Arcadia Publishing
Charleston, South Carolina

Printed in the United States of America

For all general information, please contact Arcadia Publishing:
Telephone 843-853-2070
Fax 843-853-0044
E-mail sales@arcadiapublishing.com
For customer service and orders:
Toll-Free 1-888-313-2665

Visit us on the Internet at www.arcadiapublishing.com

On the Front Cover: The River Store of E.L. Arthur at Head of the River was located on the north side of Jericho Turnpike, where the statue of Richard Smythe's legendary bull, Whisper, stands today. Owned and operated by Ethelbert Arthur, the establishment sold a variety of merchandise, lumber, and coal while also housing Smithtown's post office for a number of years. In 1912, the store and the house beside it burned to the ground. (Historic image courtesy Smithtown Historical Society; modern photograph by John DiGiacomo.)

On the Back Cover: In this photograph taken around 1900 looking south near the old Riverside Inn, Peter Hunter waters his team of workhorses on the Nissequogue River. The photographer perfectly captured the picturesque setting, with blossoms overhead in the trees on the opposite shore and a striking reflection cast across the water in the foreground. (Historic image courtesy Smithtown Historical Society.)

Contents

Acknowledgments

The authors would like to extend our profound appreciation to all the people who assisted in the creation of this book by lending their photographs, expertise, and time. There is no question that photographer John DiGiacomo belongs at the top of this list, and putting his name on the cover does not go far enough. John brought so much more than his professionalism and artistic eye to bear on the project. He also has an infectious curiosity and interest in the past, and working with him from beginning to end was a great pleasure. Beyond his careful study of the proper camera angles and distances, John took into consideration the time of day for shooting—to get the proper light and visual effect, but also borne out of some concern for personal safety. (You try standing out on Middle Country Road during rush hour to take a photograph. We dare you!)

As with our previous book, a special thank you also goes to Cathy Ball and Caren Zatyk, our friends who opened the door once again to their outstanding materials—both photographic and reference—at the Richard H. Handley Collection of Long Island Americana at the Smithtown Library. Ball and Zatyk are extremely busy with several major projects these days, and yet they typically put those demands on hold to do their very best to help us. The Handley Collection remains an extraordinary resource for genealogists and professional and amateur historians. Several of that collection's photographs are published in this volume.

Our gratitude also goes to Walter Macheck, Lee Corbani, David Thompson, Carole Nelson, Patricia McManus Ward, the Kings Park Heritage Museum, Carole Palmer, Steve Gallagher, and Greg Gottlieb and the Hauppauge Fire Department for lending or facilitating the rights to publish images. Father Jack Custer from the Resurrection Byzantine Catholic Church answered some important questions about his church's history. We would also like to thank the numerous individuals who saw the value in what we were doing and allowed us to take pictures of their residences and business establishments.

Finally, we thank our families for stoically being our sounding boards to all things Smithtown, ferrying us to and fro, and patiently putting up with more than a few early mornings and late evenings as we pieced this puzzle together.

Unless otherwise noted, all of the historic images in the book are from the collection of the Smithtown Historical Society. All of the modern images were taken by John DiGiacomo.

Introduction

Writing of New York City in the 1840s, ex-mayor and famous diarist Philip Hoyne decried its unremitting pace of change: "Overturn, overturn, overturn! Is the maxim of New York. The very bones of our ancestors are not permitted to lie quiet a quarter of a century, and one generation of men seem studious to remove all relics of those who preceded him." Smithtown in 2011 shares both the bustling nature and the seeming obsession with transition that so incensed Hone. Walking down Main Street in the village or driving over any main thoroughfare through the town tends to reinforce the feeling that the only thing constant about the place is that it will look different tomorrow. We may be permitted to ask ourselves if the Smithtown we know, where we eat, play, pray, do business, and go to school, will have any resemblance to that future place inherited by our children and grandchildren.

Our previous book, *Smithtown* (2009), did not ignore that contemporary perspective but did often dwell in the town's illustrated historic past. This new book gave the authors and our skillful, historic-minded photographer, John DiGiacomo, a chance to have one foot in both dimensions of time. It also allowed us to go beyond our daily impressions and to really catalog and document the measure of change on Smithtown's landscape and built environment over the decades. The process was at once fascinating, exhilarating, and troublesome. One thing we did not anticipate was that obtaining a modern view of the exact same location 75 to 120 years later is sometimes utterly impossible. Trees grow (or are axed down), as do traffic overpasses, new commercial buildings, and the width and breadth of roadways. One example: a beautifully scenic c. 1910 view looking down a rolling hill towards the old Miller estate had no modern analogue. Today's view is completely blocked by utility wires and the backside of Main Street's retail district (see page 79).

The process of choosing comparative vantage points for this book was primarily refined by consulting available historic photographs and making visits to the actual locations. Most of the "then" photographs in this book came from the Smithtown Historical Society's collection, with a smaller number of pictures included from individuals and several other institutions. We also attempted to spread even geographic distribution throughout our book. This is no easy task with Smithtown, a township of approximately 55 square miles encompassing 10 incorporated villages and hamlets. Despite our efforts, it should not be surprising that there are more images from Smithtown and Smithtown Branch in this book than any other area of the township, as a result of the town's historic settlement pattern and the focus of the collections we drew from.

When did "old" Smithtown begin becoming new? When did *then* morph into *now*? There is no one easy or satisfying answer to those questions, only a series of markers and clues in the historical record. Certainly the period of the 1950s and early 1960s was the era of the most rapid change. Smithtown's population grew 57 percent from 1960 to 1964 alone. Realizing that this huge demographic shift had enormous fiscal and physical implications, the town hired planner T.T. McCrosky to review the area and write a consulting plan in 1957. In proposing the preservation of additional green space and parkland, he stated that "for those who have striven to stay one jump ahead of the monotonous miles of houses in Queens and Nassau Counties, it must be obvious that people who are banded together into communities must make a stand against the onslaught. How high should the goal be set? Only the residents of Smithtown can answer this question. Their answer will be measured by their willingness to accept the financial responsibility of these parklands in terms of taxes and donations." The town adopted many of McCrosky's recommendations in its 1961 master plan, and in future decades, many pushed for the addition of parks and the preservation of the town's historic buildings.

Although maintenance of its scenic and historic character has been a chief town priority, there is often a distance between such sensible aims and the reality of their implementation. Time marches forward, and new demands always come to the fore. Hopefully our books can offer more than just a sentimental paean to the way things were. We would like to inspire the same wonder at Smithtown's past that we ourselves have, as well as a call to act and preserve, to deny the drive to "remove all relics" of those who came before.

CHAPTER

HOMEBOUND

HOUSES DESTROYED, MOVED, PRESERVED

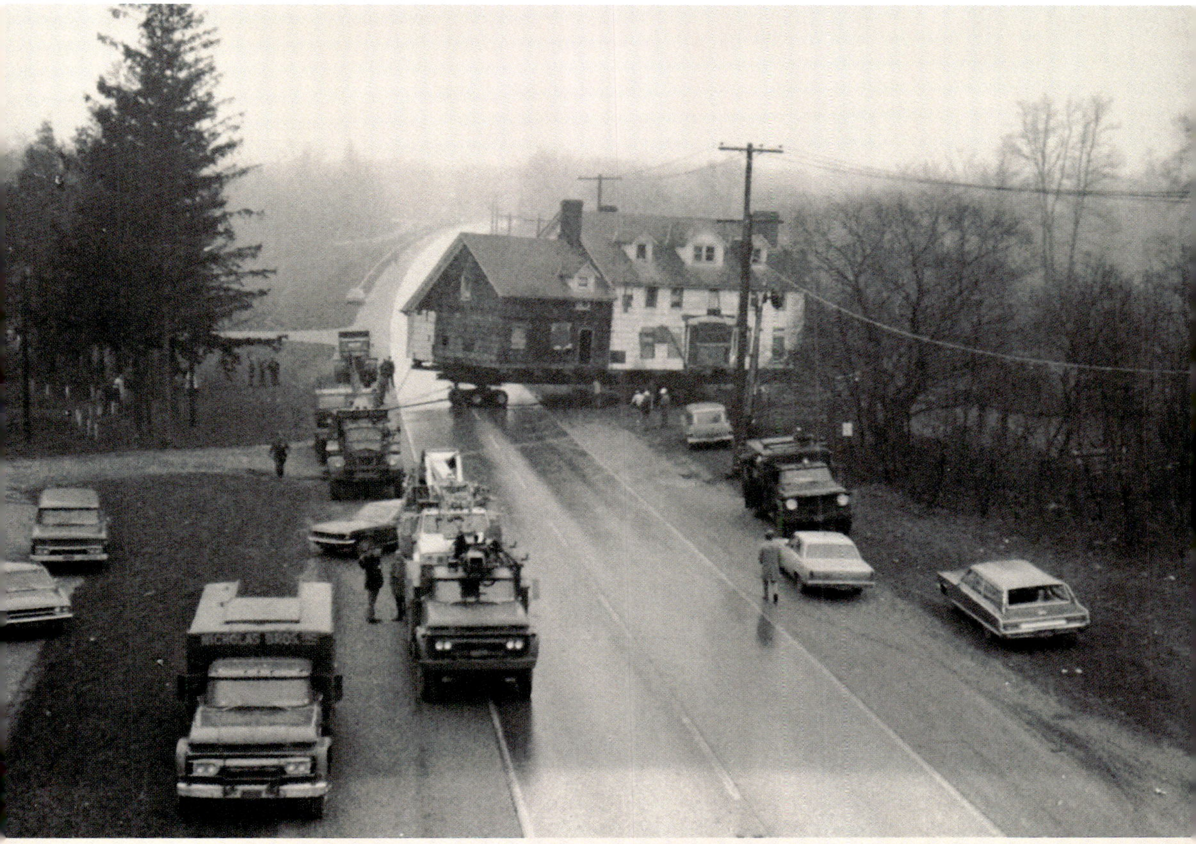

In 1972, the historic Epenetus Smith Tavern was threatened with demolition until the Smithtown Branch Preservation Association came to the rescue, purchasing the tavern for $1 and arranging to have it moved. Davis Movers jacked up the huge building, placed steel beams beneath it, put the house on wheels, and hauled it to its present location on Middle Country Road.

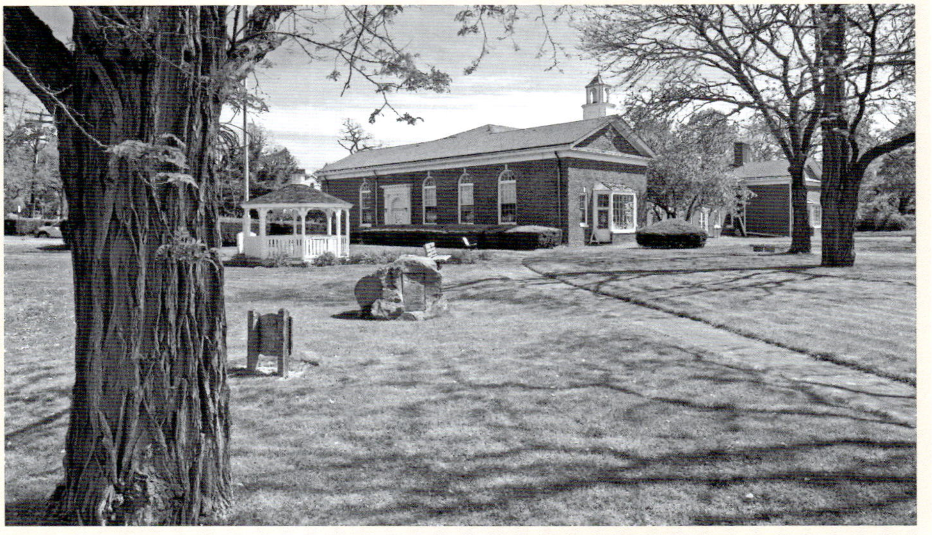

Built in the early 1700s, Widow Blydenburgh's Tavern graced the northeast corner of Middle Country Road and North Country Road until it was razed in the early 1900s. In 1923, the newly created Village Green Corporation acquired the property in hopes of maintaining it as a public park. The town's gradual loss of interest in the site prompted the organization to donate the land to the Smithtown Library in 1947. A plaque-emblazoned boulder has commemorated the historic tavern's location since 1932.

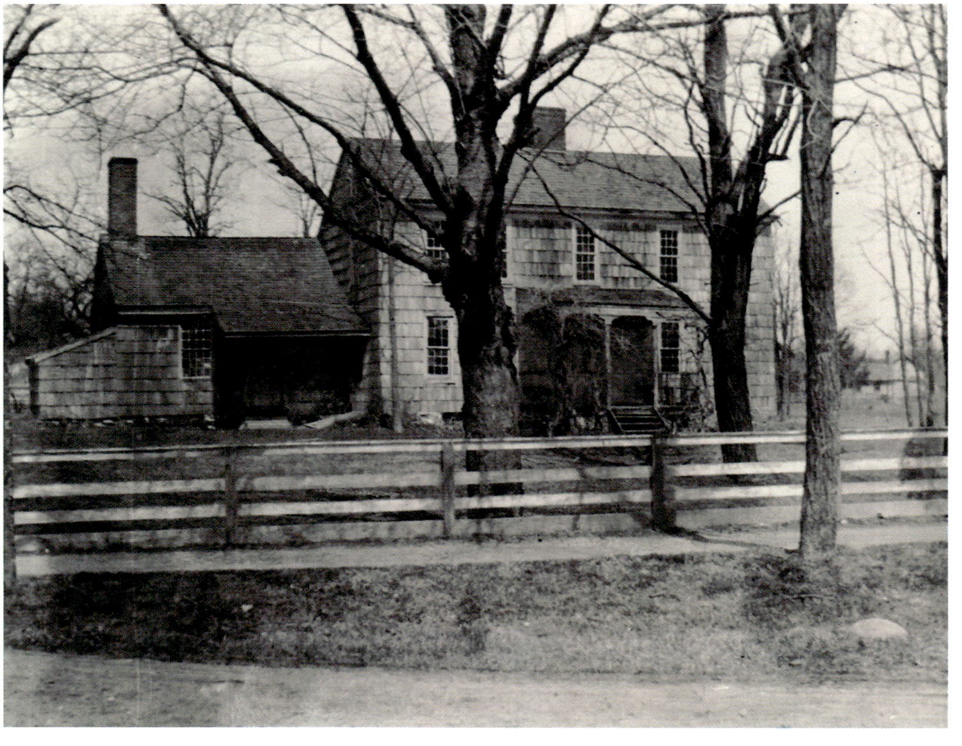

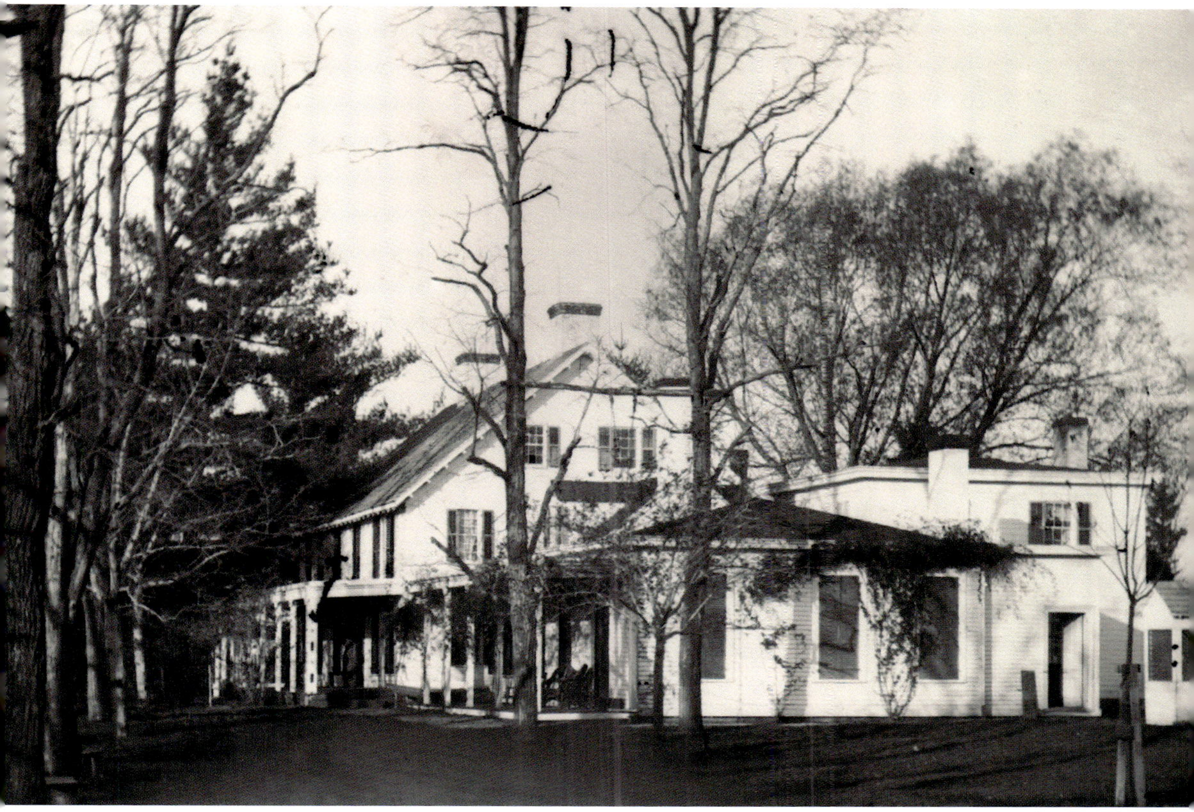

Still informally known by Smithtown residents as "the Homestead," this beautiful white house at 205 Middle Country Road was built in the 1760s and owned principally by the Blydenburgh and Smith families before becoming part of the Smithtown Historical Society's collection. Added onto substantially on its east facade by Judge John Lawrence Smith, the house was once surrounded by a plethora of outbuildings on its grounds (several of which still exist).

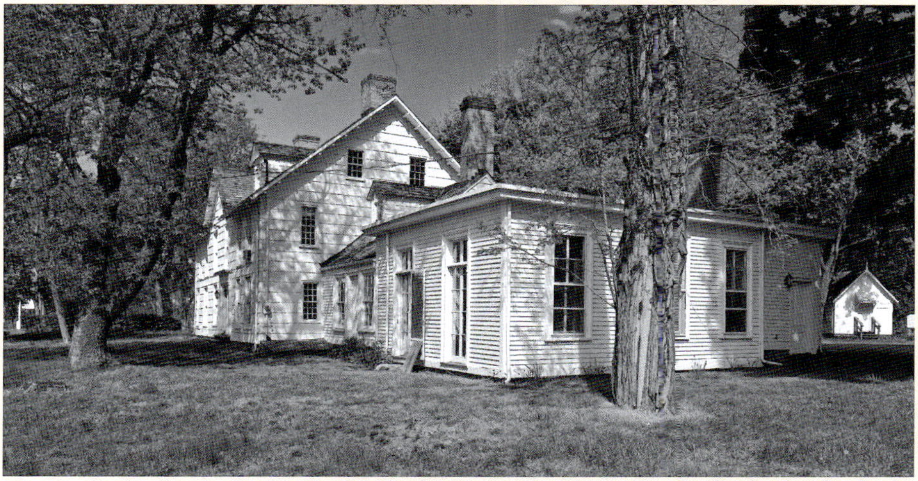

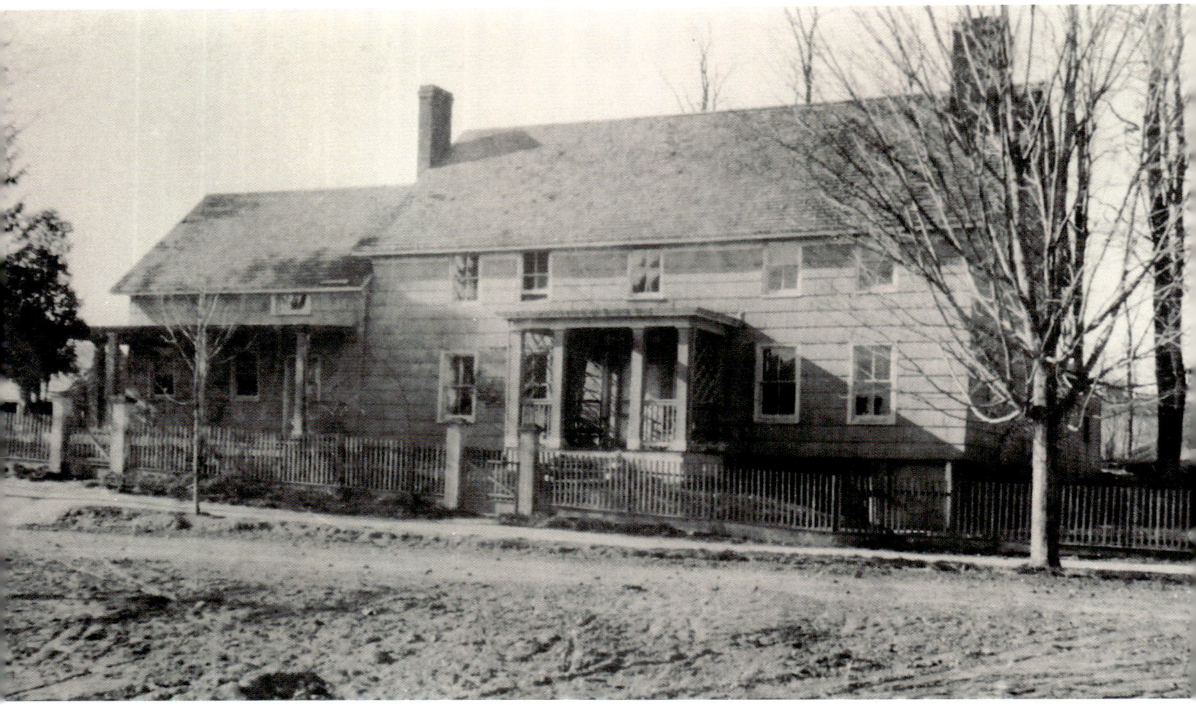

The Epenetus Smith Tavern is seen here on its original site, west of the Presbyterian church, across from the road to Hauppauge (Singer Lane). The historic tavern (its earliest wing dates to around 1690) has been moved three times in its life: first in 1911 to the west side of Route 111, then subsequently across Route 111, where it served as a restaurant for a number of years, and finally to its present home, 211 Middle Country Road, in 1972.

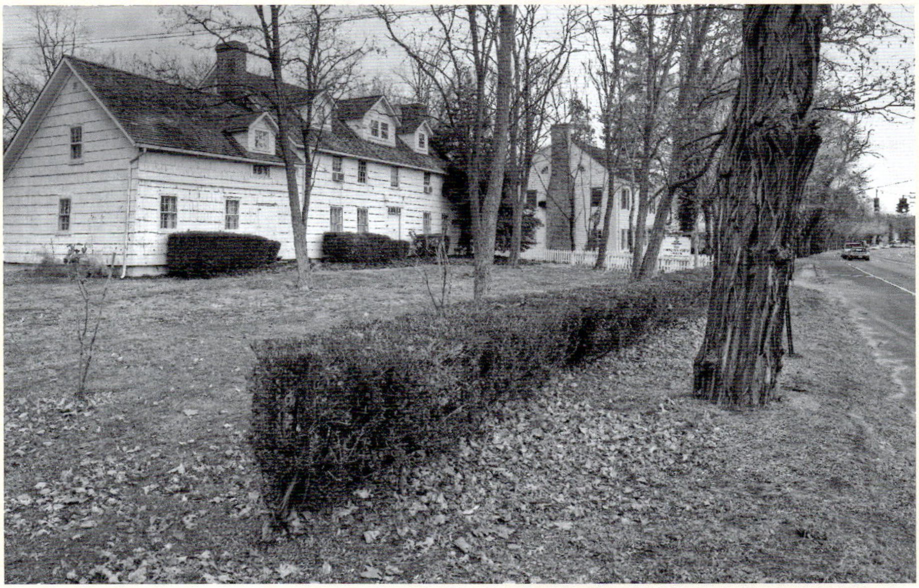

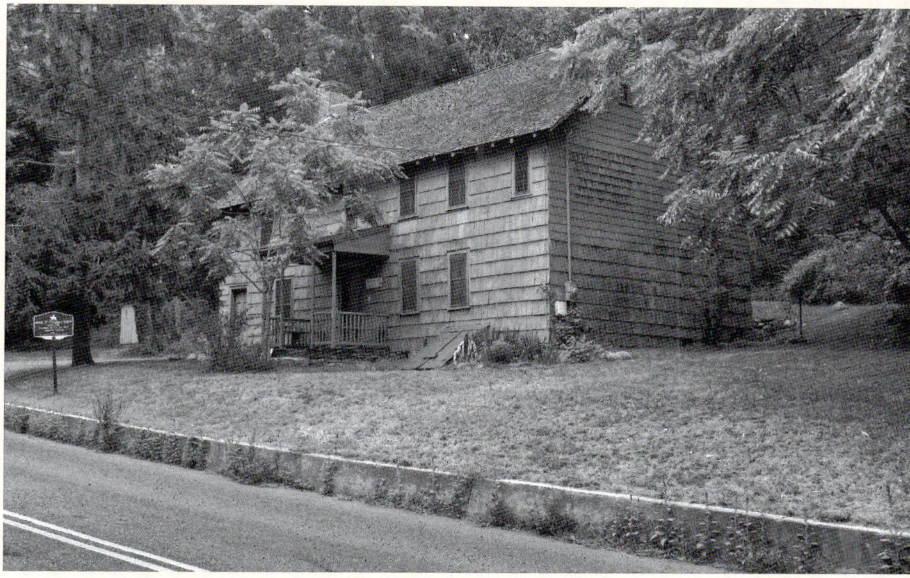

Built at what is now 853 St. Johnland Road in the early 1700s, the Obadiah Smith House is the oldest structure located on the west bank of the Nissequogue River. The house, named for the grandson of town patentee Richard Smythe, remained in the Smith family until 1834. In 1960, the Smithtown Historical Society acquired the home and began the task of preserving it to be used for the public's benefit and enjoyment—a purpose it still serves today.

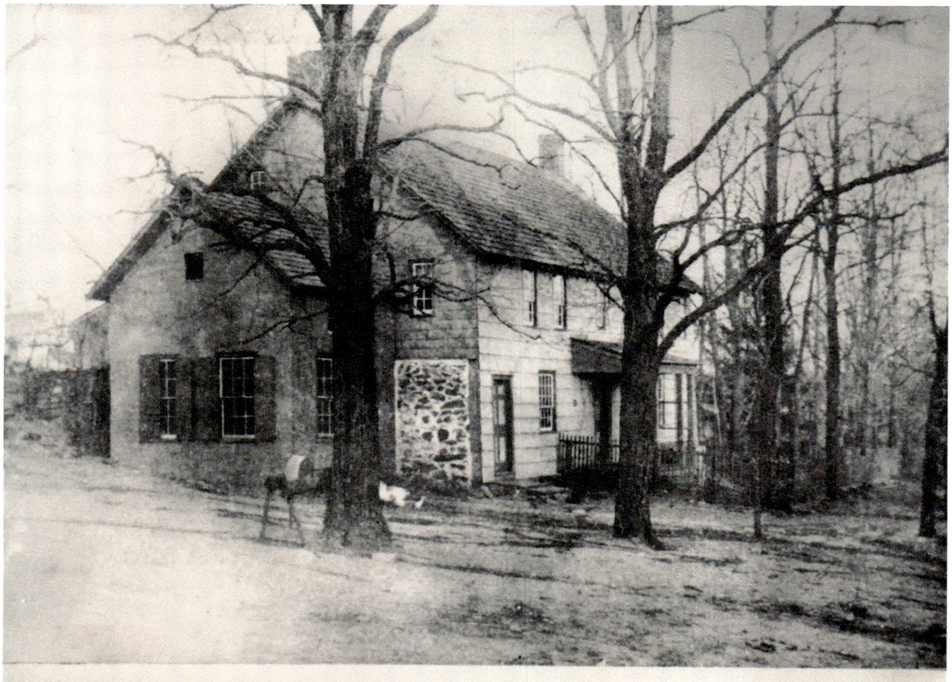

The Obadiah Smith House photographed around 1880.

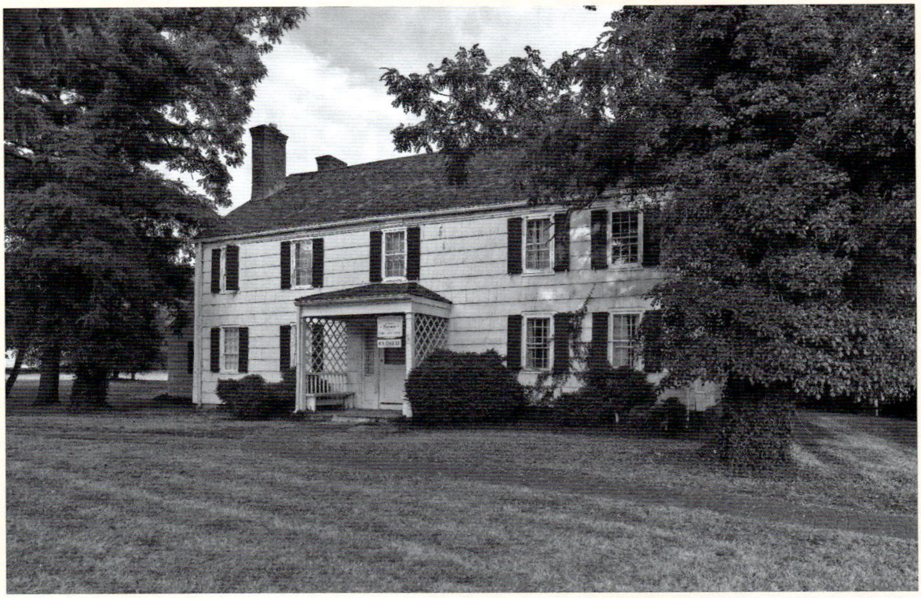

The main part of the structure was built in 1819 for Caleb Smith II. Set to be demolished to make way for a new development in 1955, the home's incredible 13-mile move from Commack to its present site in Smithtown was funded by the original owner's great-granddaughter Anna Blydenburgh. Crews from the power and telephone utility companies cleared the lines as three trucks and tractors moved the structure and its roof separately.

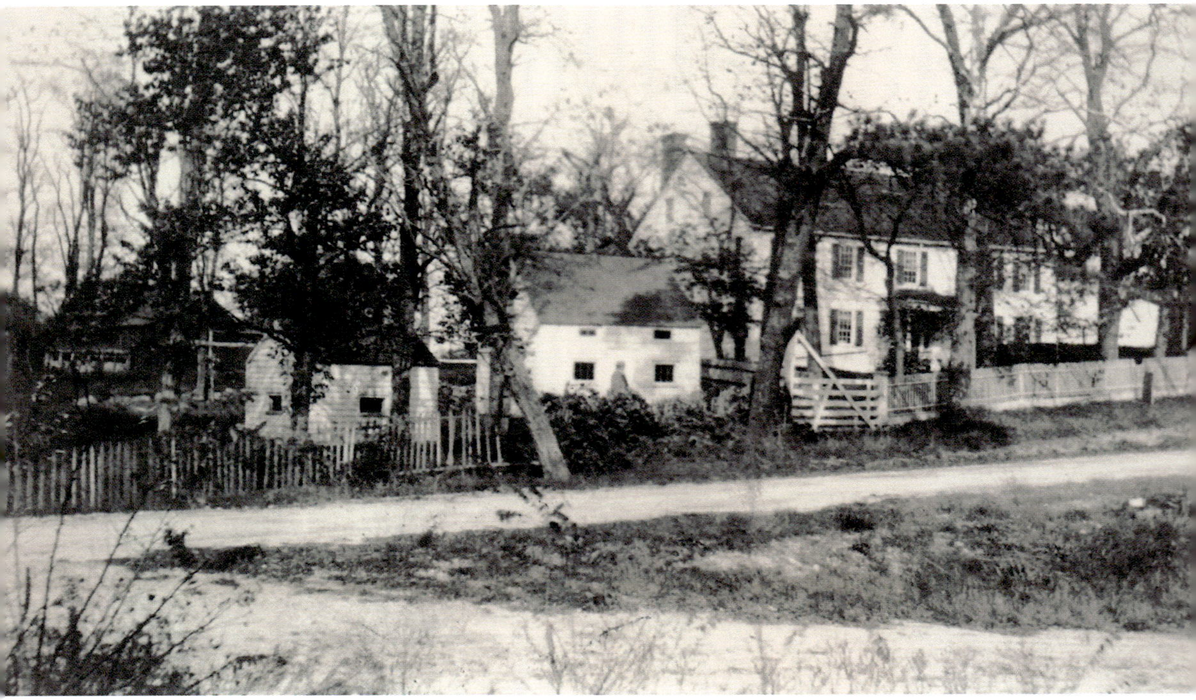

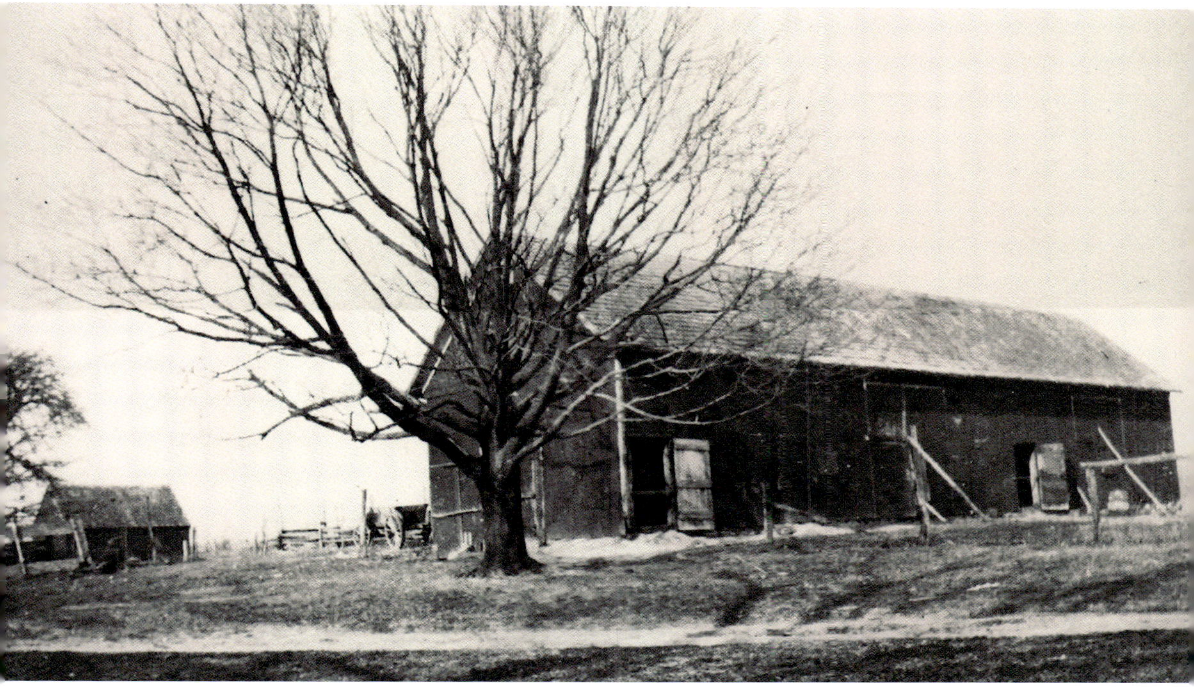

While the main house was saved, all of the outbuildings—including this barn—were leveled. The most unique structure on the property that was lost was a simple one-and-a-half-story cottage that had been quarters for slaves and later servants of the Smith family. Photographed in 1915, this barn was sitting in the middle of surrounding potato fields that stretched as far away as the eye could see. Today, a bowling alley occupies the site.

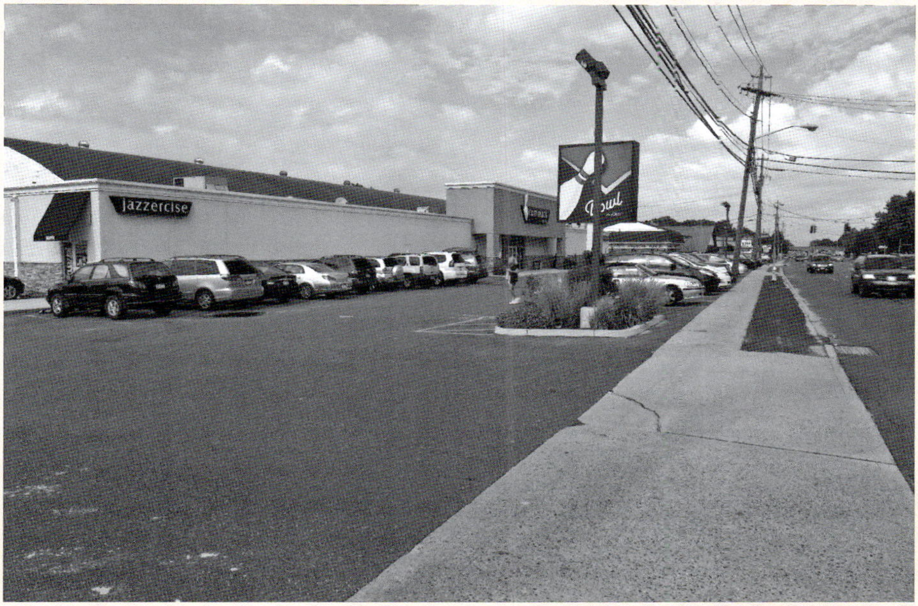

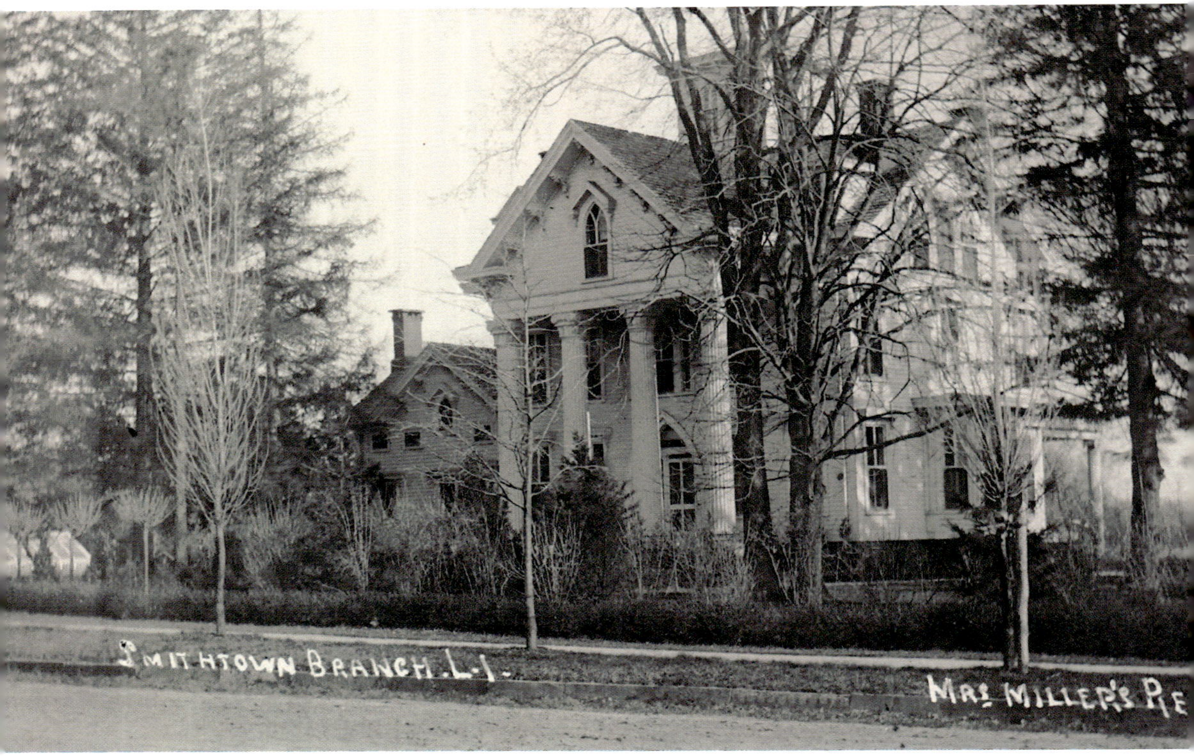

When this historic photograph was taken, Mary Ely Miller owned the house and over 100 acres of property extending from Lawrence Avenue to Singer Lane and south from Main Street to Miller's Pond. Actively farmed in the 1940s, the property was sold to developers in 1953, allowing for the construction of the Smithtown Shopping Center along Main Street. The Miller House stood abandoned until it was torn down in the 1960s to make way for the Branch Shopping Center.

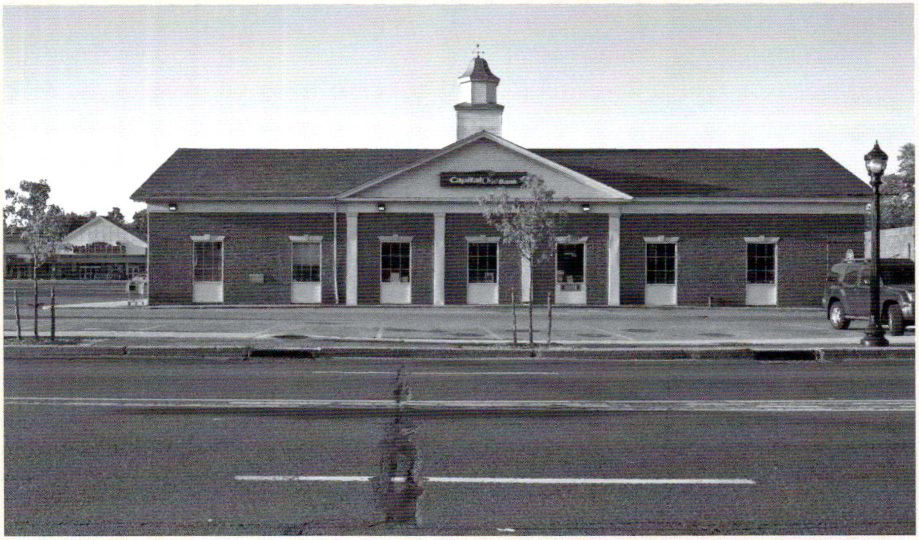

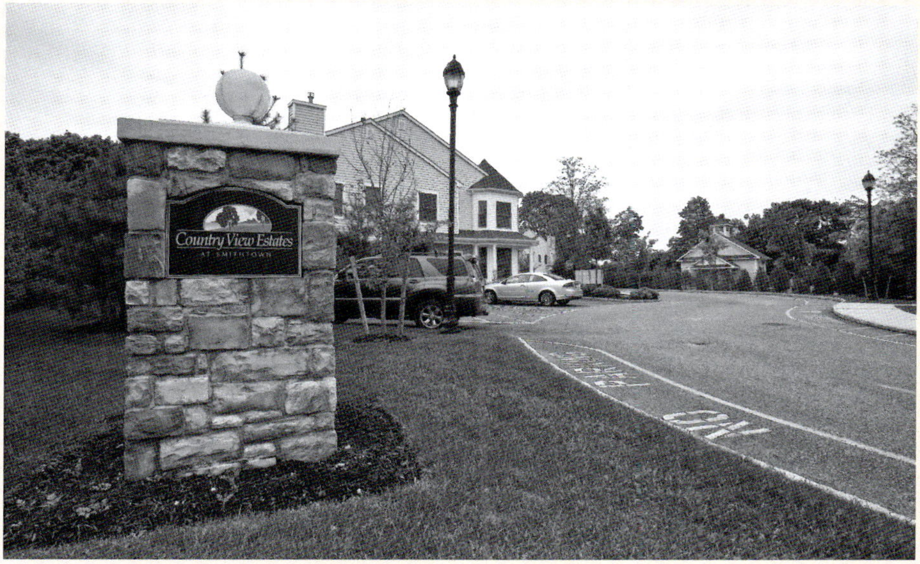

Clinton B. Darling lived and ran his undertaking business at this home on Landing Avenue in Smithtown Branch, seen here in 1904. The business was established by his father, Emmet W. Darling, in 1874. When his father died in 1904, Clinton Darling carried it on until his own death in 1947. His former home was soon sold, becoming the Little Gift Shop. In 1988, the house and property were sold again, the house was demolished, and condominiums were built on the site.

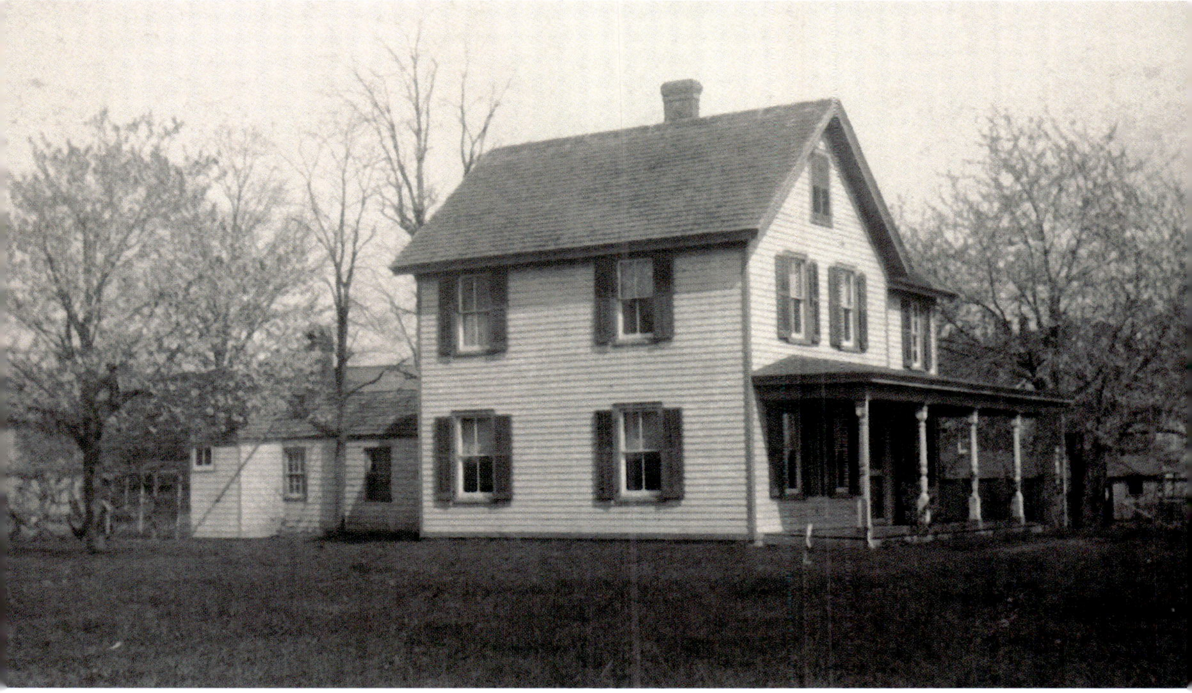

This house on the northeast corner of Landing and Blydenburgh Avenues was built in 1892 by Theodore Willis Smith when he moved to Smithtown Branch to start an insurance business. After his death in 1918, his only daughter, Faith Smith, lived here and continued the business. Faith Smith was one of Smithtown's more active businesswomen, running her insurance agency until she was 76. She lived in this house until her death in December 1976 at the age of 93.

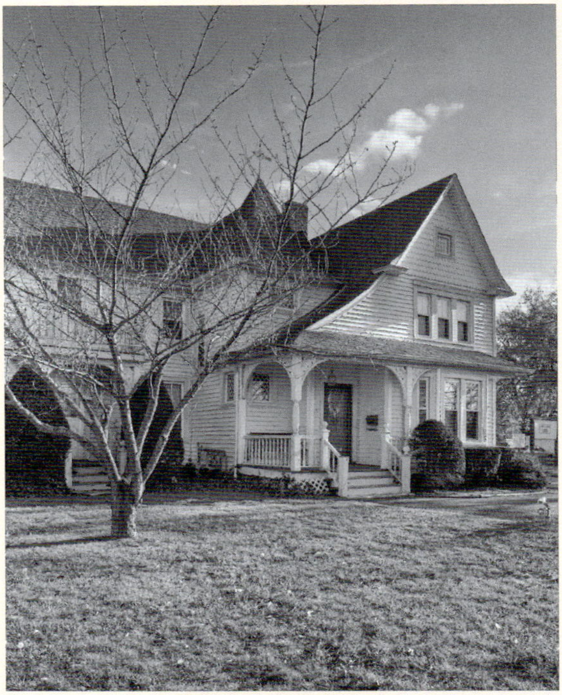

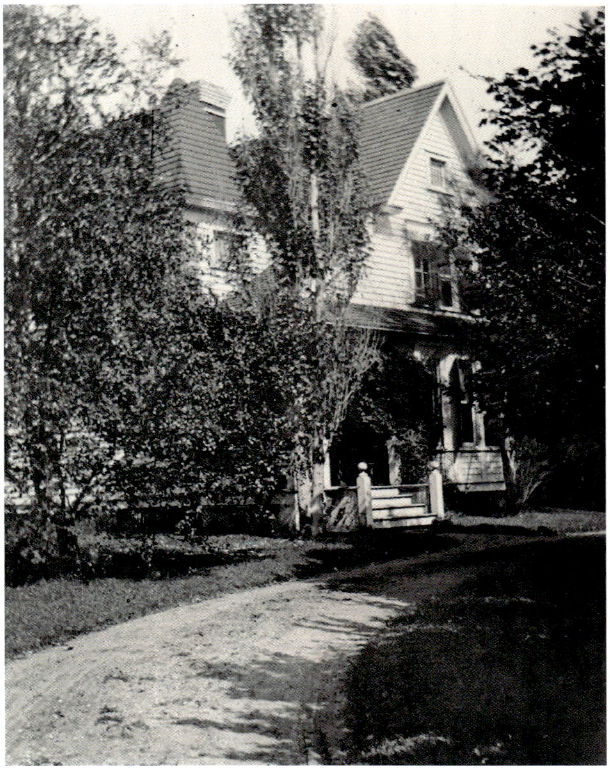

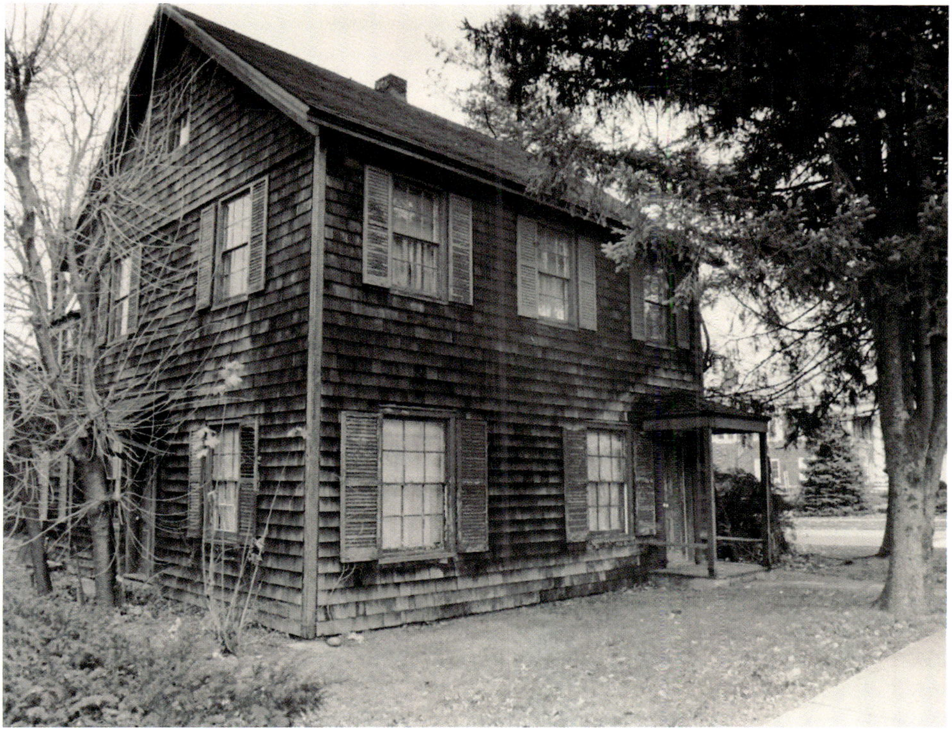

This house, on the corner of Redwood Lane and Main Street, was home to three generations of the Scott family. Arriving in Smithtown Branch in 1898, Walter F. Scott moved into this house and began a plumbing business. Scott operated the business until he retired in 1935, passing the shop to his son, Earl Scott, who subsequently left it to his son, Donald Scott. The Scott House and plumbing shop are now owned by the Evergreen Mortgage Company.

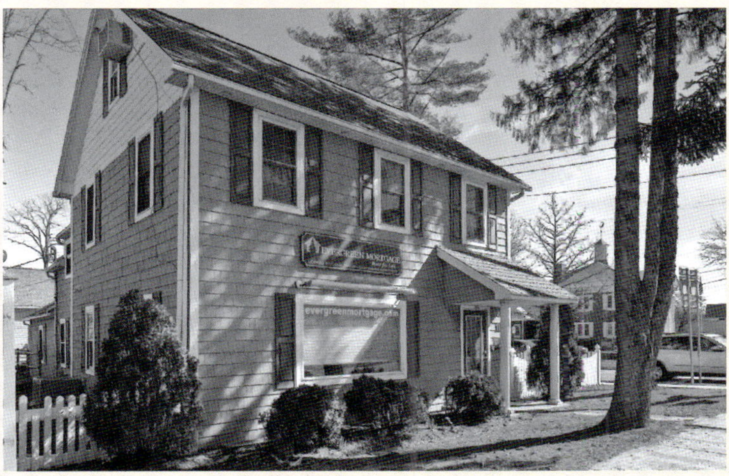

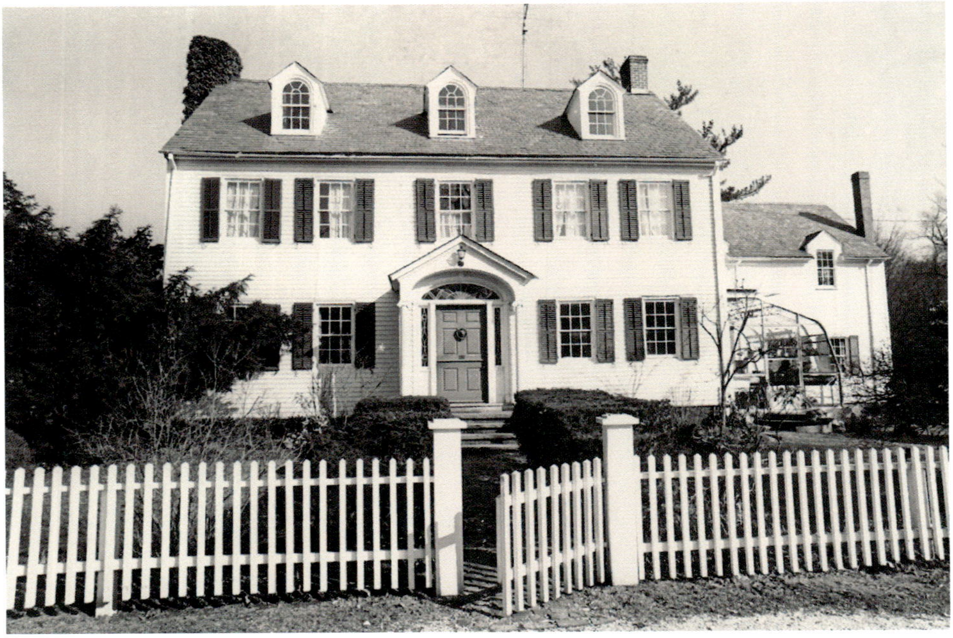

Built prior to 1795, when Moses and Isaac Mills purchased the home, the Treadwell-Wheeler House played host to a general store until the Wheeler family acquired it in 1848. During the Wheeler family's 60 years of ownership, the house was renovated and expanded. After another 50 years of subsequent owners and remodeling, Lyman and Beth Watt purchased the house in 1958 and lived there for the next 40 years before selling it to its current owners.

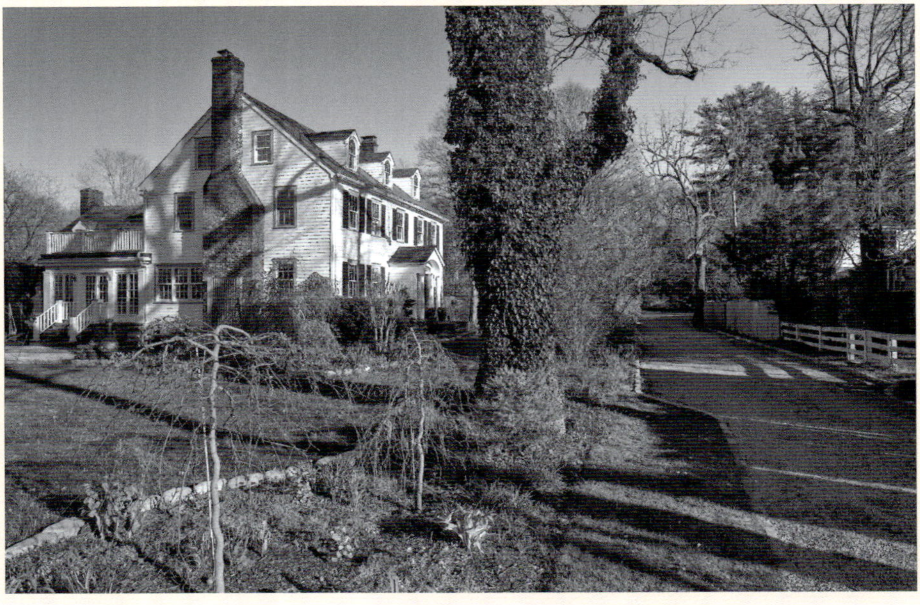

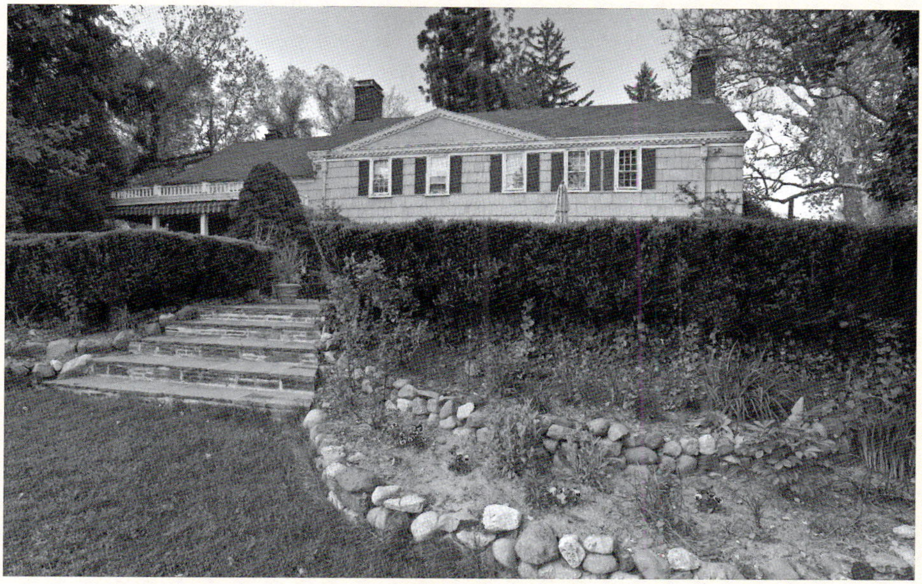

The Phillips House was built some time prior to 1726, the year that George Phillips came to live in Head of the River. The split-level house was used as a residence, tavern, store, and Smithtown's first post office. Located in what was then the center of the village of Smithtown, the structure was home to four generations of the Phillips family, proprietors of the gristmill, sawmill, and fulling mill located on the dam across the Nissequogue River.

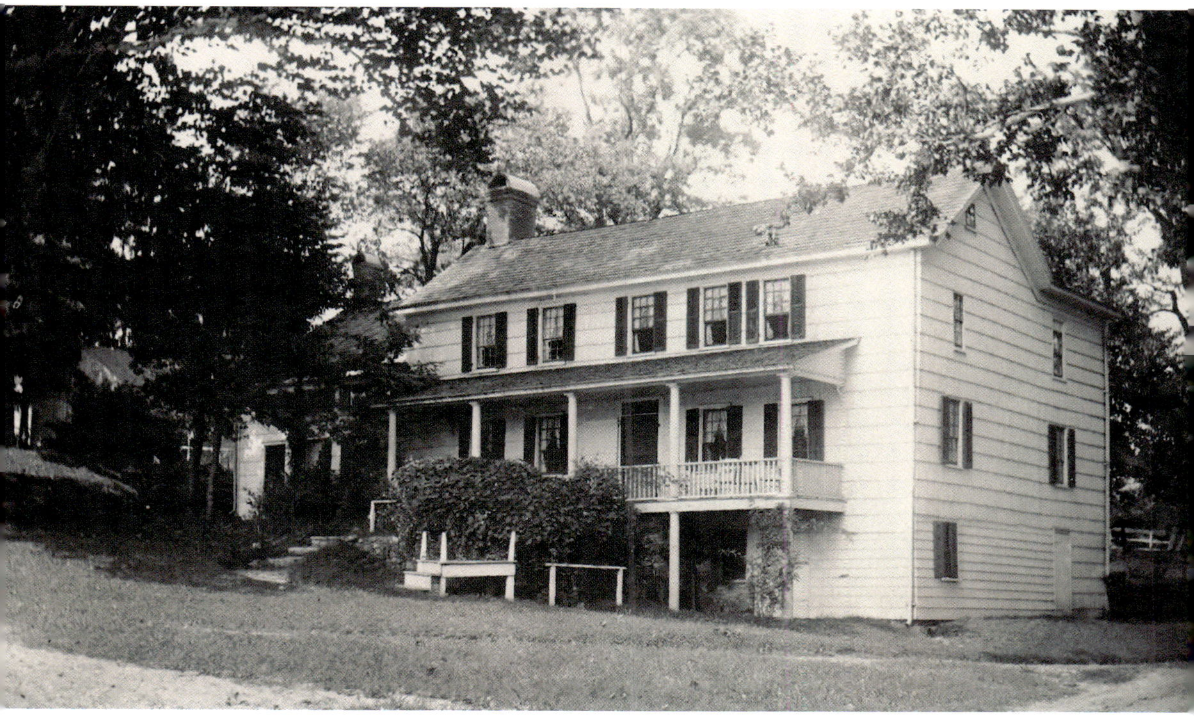

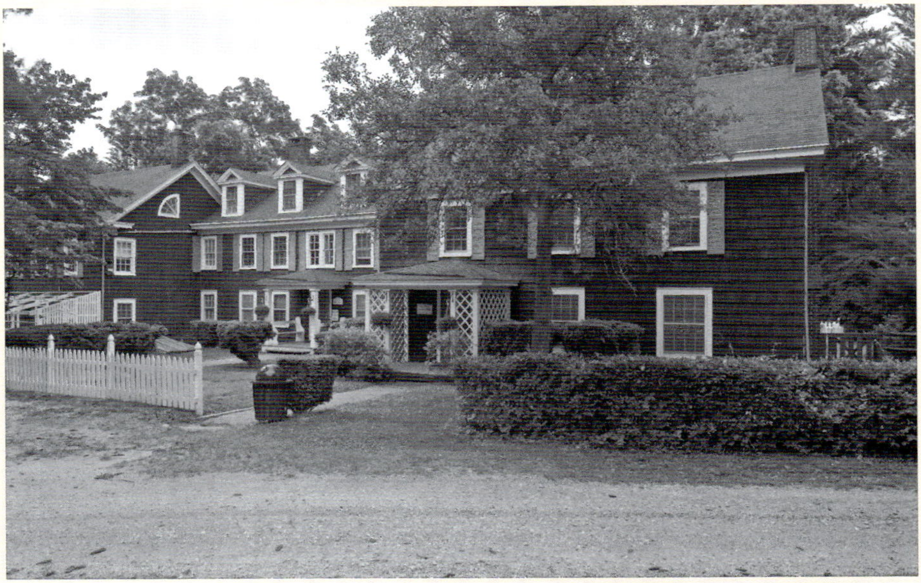

In 1910, Edwin and Maria Hoyt purchased the Wickes family's 300-acre farm in southern Commack as a vacation home. By 1920, Hoyt had planted 5,000 apple trees and 15,000 peach trees and was selling the produce to local and New York City markets. The Hoyts operated their orchard for 40 years and made the farm their retirement home. In 1966, the Town of Smithtown purchased the site, seen here around 1917, and created Hoyt Farm Park.

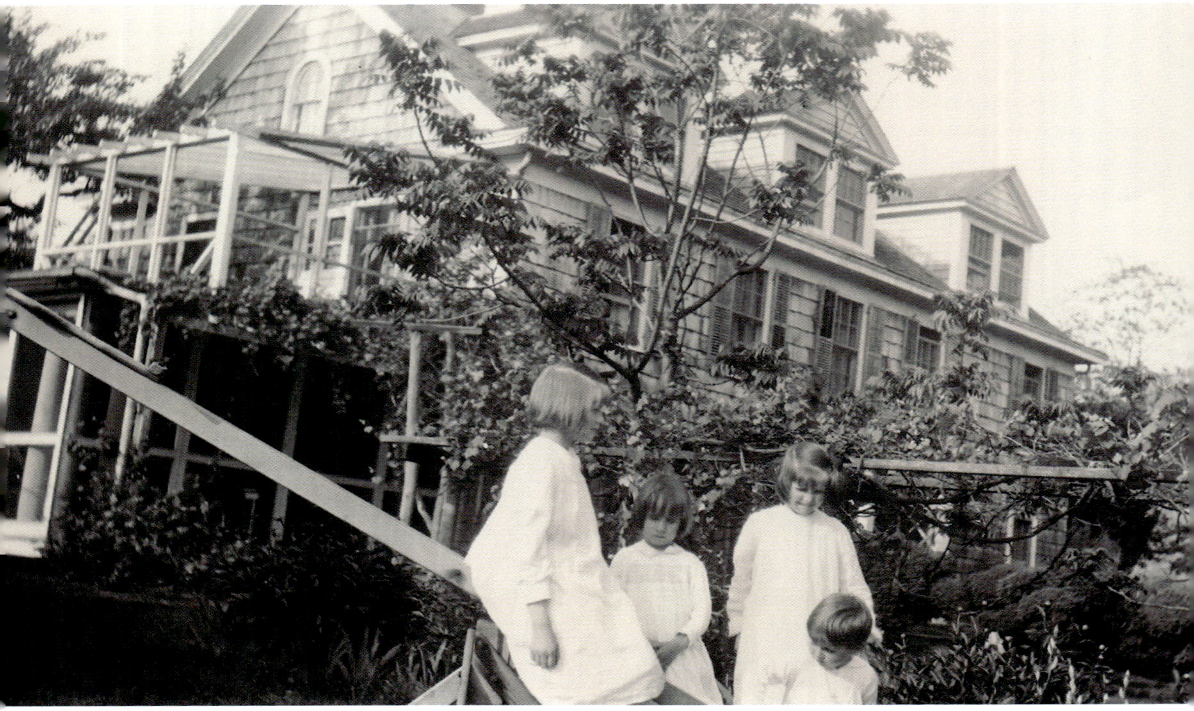

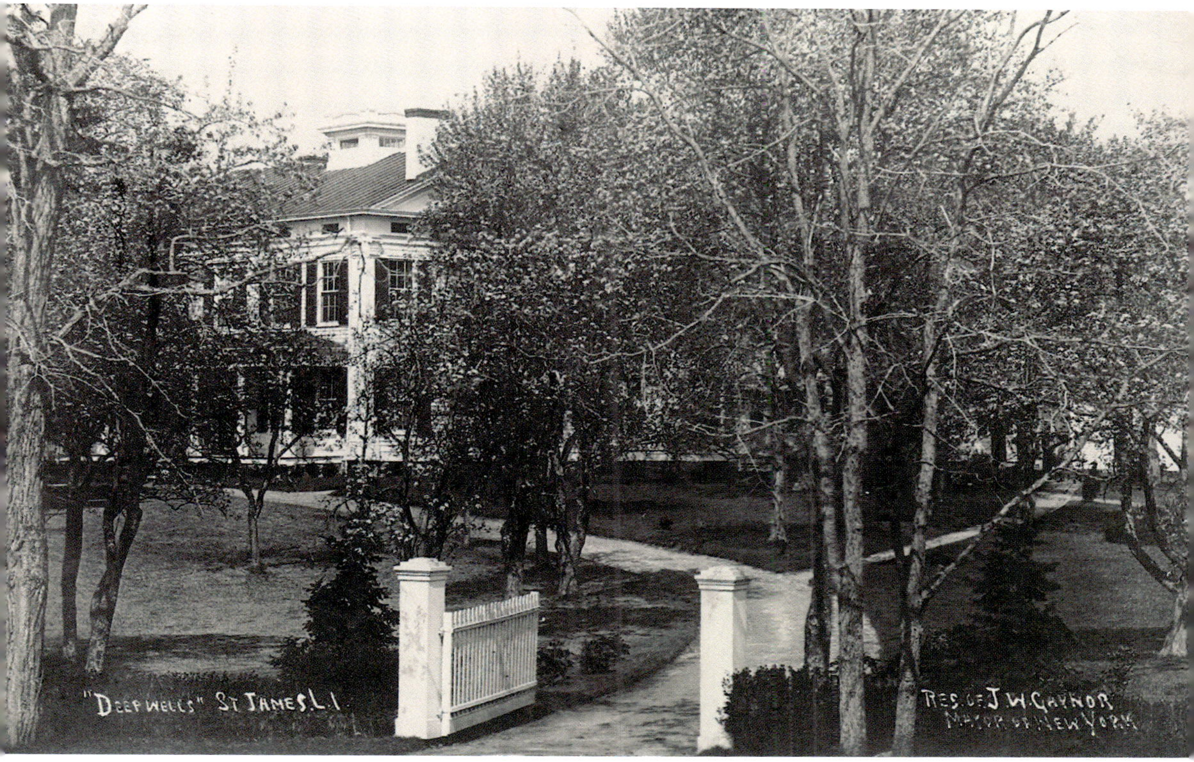

Built by Joel L.G. Smith in 1845 as part of a nearly 50-acre farm site, Deepwells Mansion takes its name from the 125-foot wells located on the property. Though the house underwent a significant renovation project during the 1920s, the site has managed to maintain many of its original characteristics. Since being acquired by Suffolk County in 1989, the estate has been preserved and kept open to the public with the help of the all-volunteer Deepwells Historical Society.

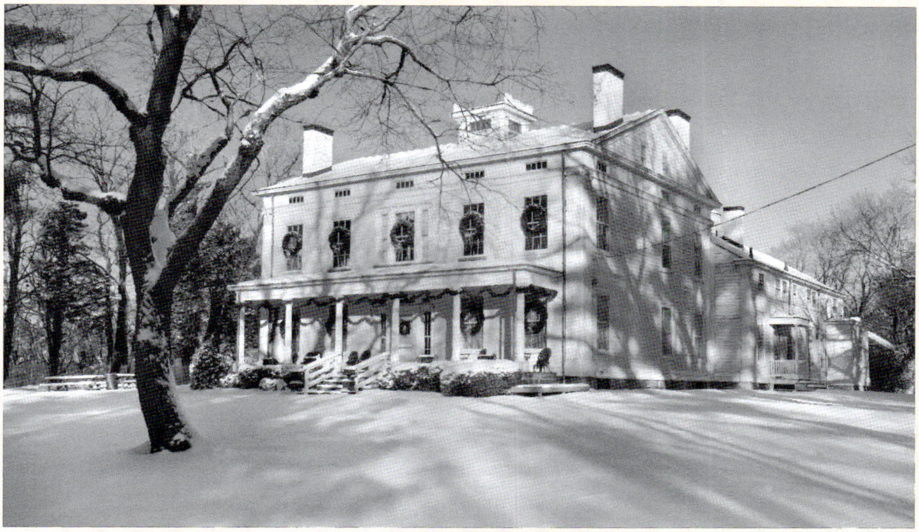

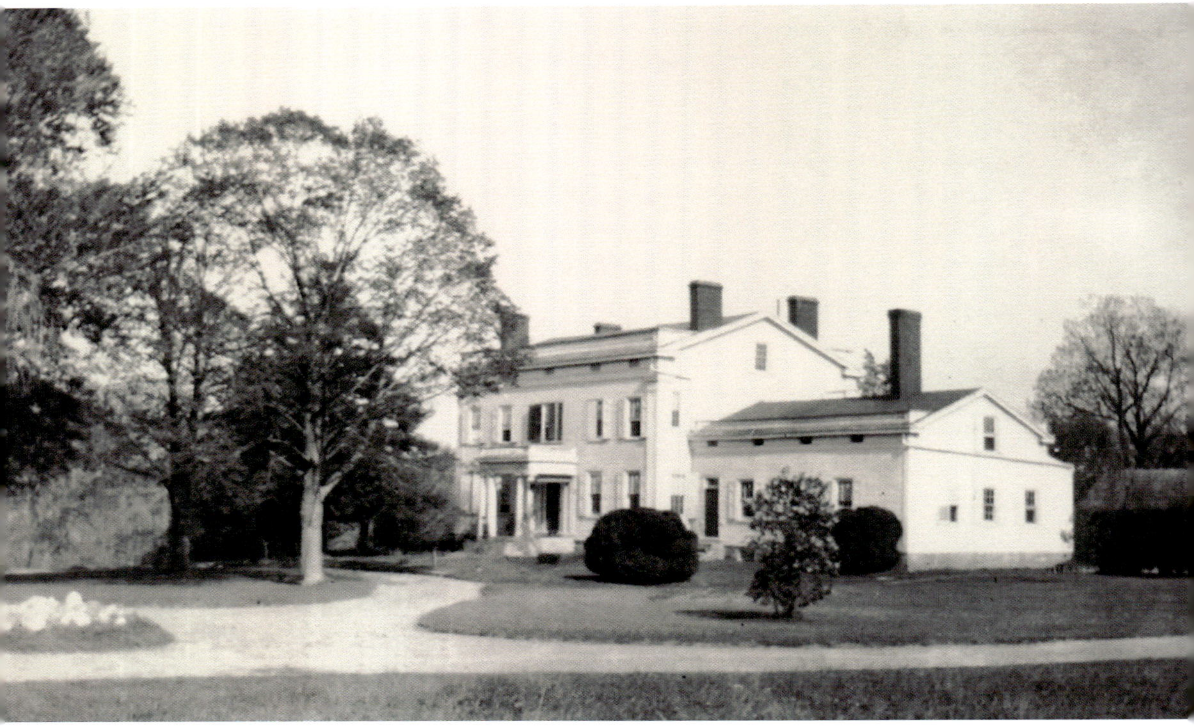

Timothy Mills built the first structure located at 660 Route 25A some time after he acquired the property in 1693. That original dwelling, though partially destroyed by fire, was restored and is incorporated into the current iteration of the Mills Pond House, which was constructed by William Wickham Mills in 1838. In 1976, descendants of the Mills family gave the home to the Town of Smithtown, and since 1978, it has served as the headquarters of the Smithtown Township Arts Council.

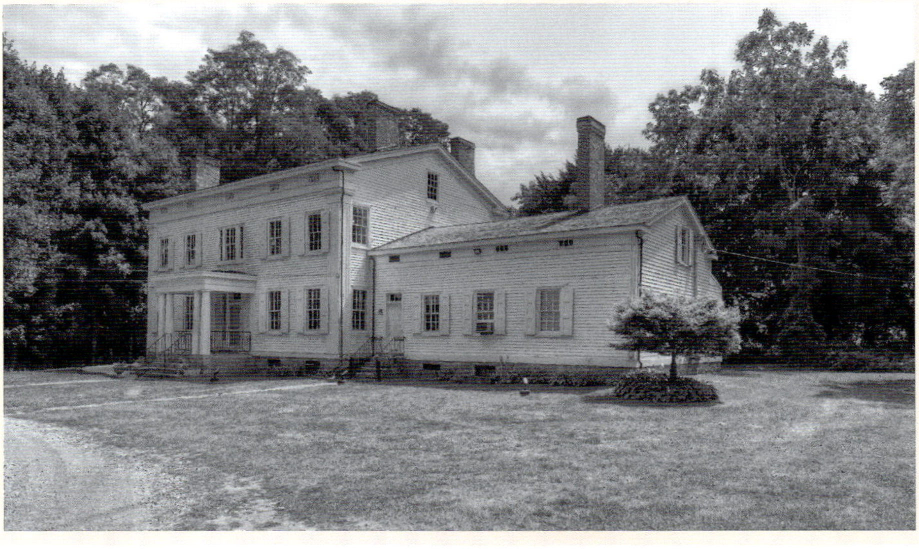

CHAPTER

NATURE'S BOUNTY

LAND AND WATERSIDE

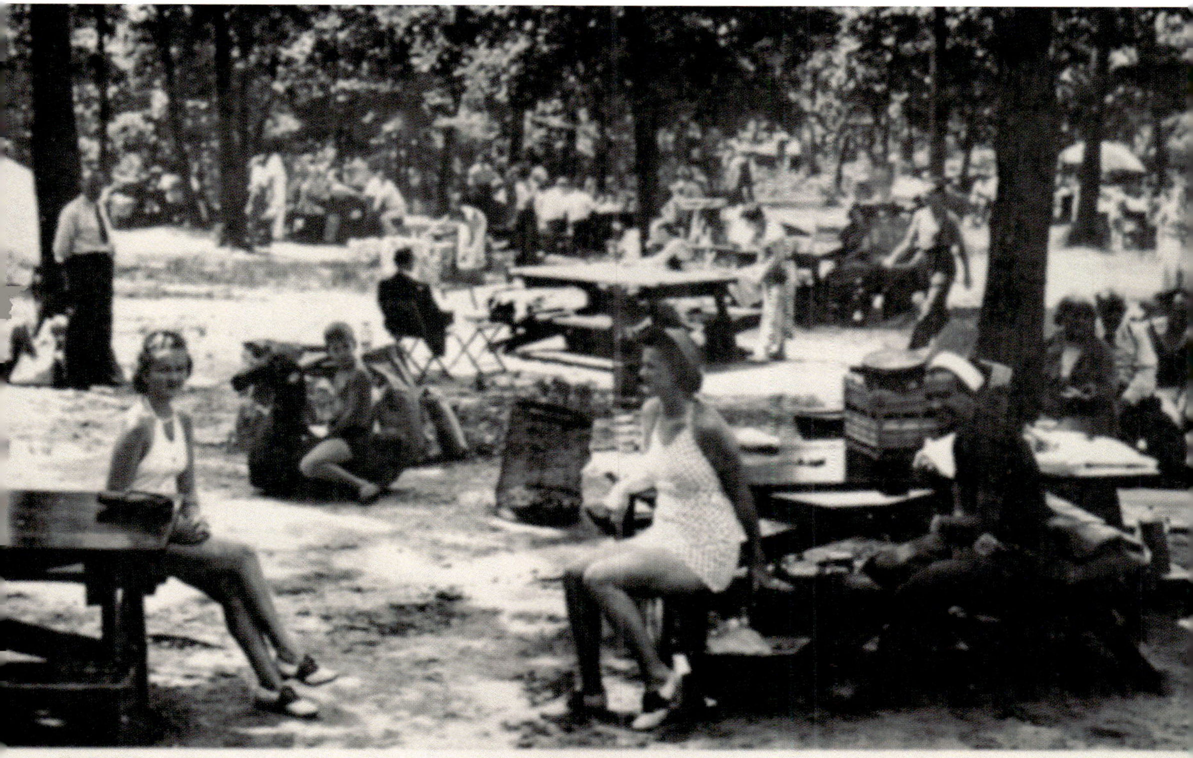

Sunken Meadow State Park was created in 1928, when the Town of Smithtown deeded over 400 acres of Long Island Sound–front property to the State of New York. Consistently among the most popular destinations in Smithtown (as evidenced by this postcard), the addition of nearly 1,000 acres of property in the 1950s only added to the site's appeal.

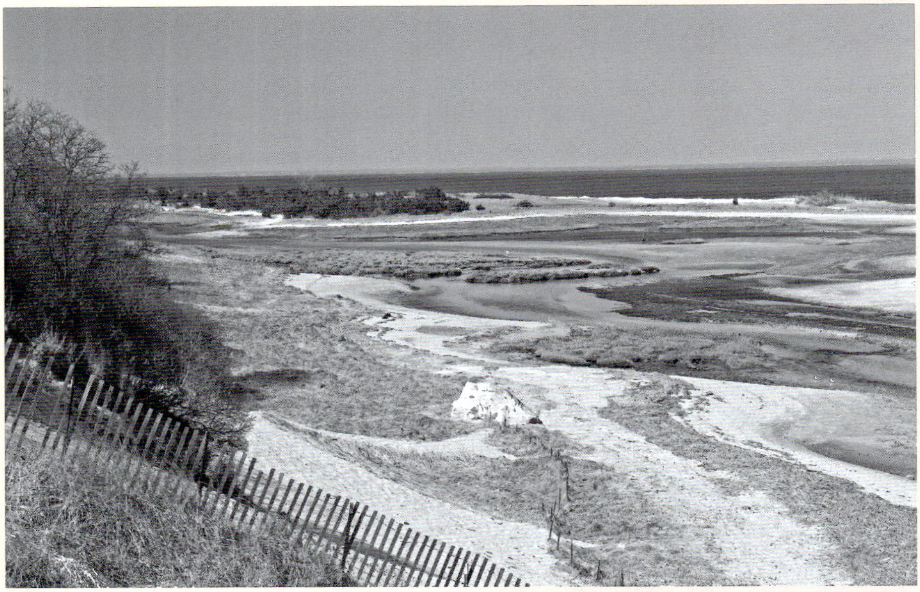

Founded with six tents and three summerhouses in 1927, the Society of St. Johnland created Camp Sandy on Plum Island to serve as a vacation spot where its boys and girls could spend the lazy, hazy days of summer. Seen here in 1935, the island was created by the confluence of Long Island Sound, Sunken Meadow Creek, and the Nissequogue River. In 1952, the land was seized through eminent domain to be incorporated into Sunken Meadow State Park.

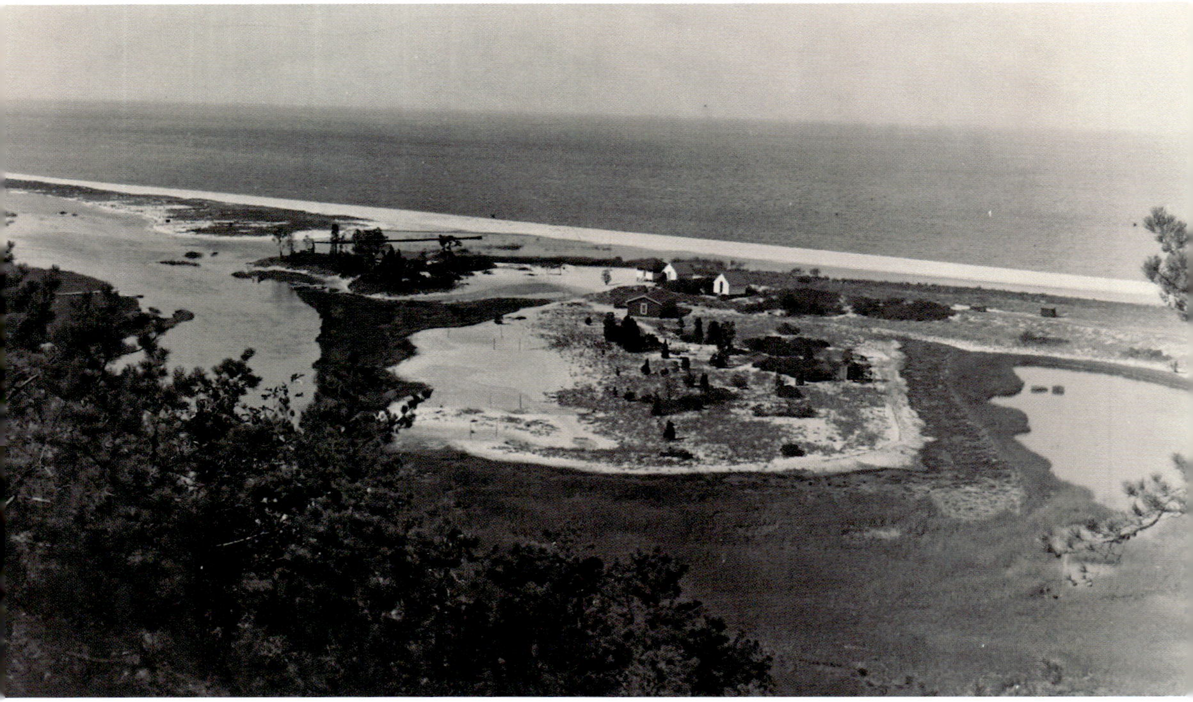

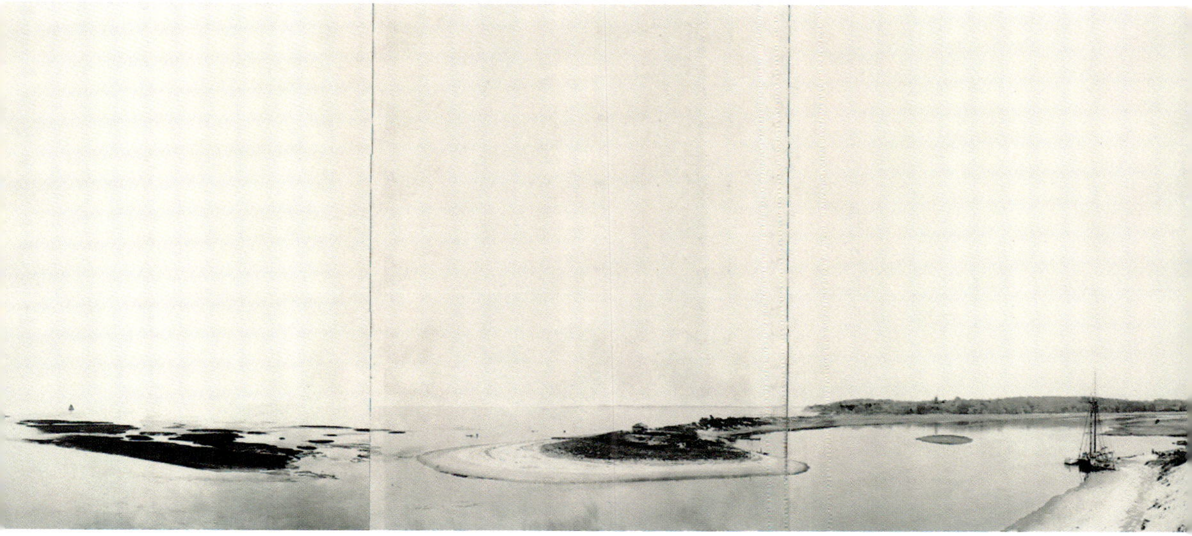

The Nissequogue River empties into the Long Island Sound, passing through Nissequogue Harbor and Sunken Meadow Creek at this very location, which became a public town beach in 1907. The complex fauna of this spot supports a diverse range of wildlife and shorebirds. Despite the seemingly timeless beauty, people may be surprised to know that, due to tidal currents, this spit of land has grown significantly westward over the past 100 years.

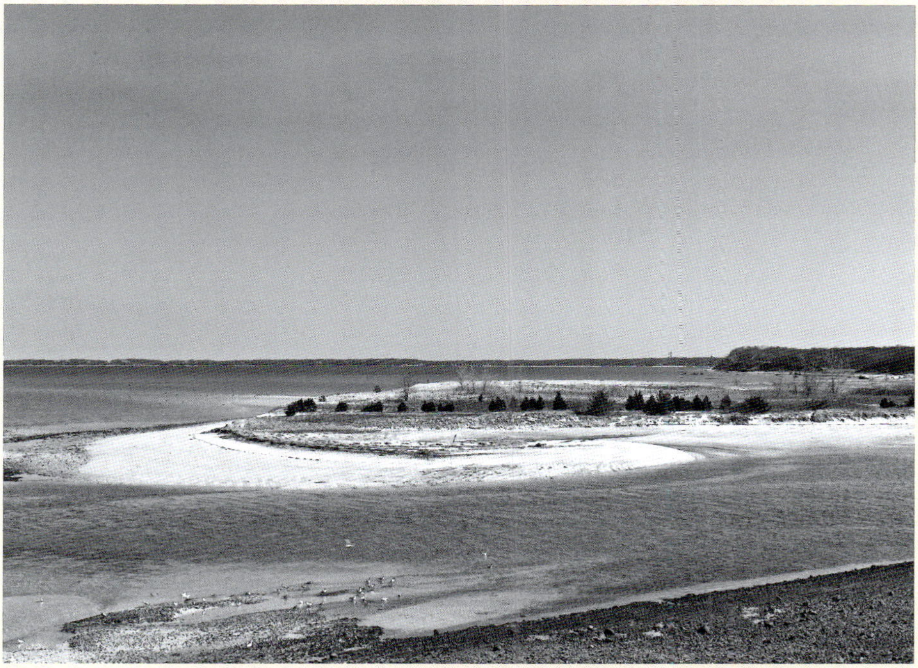

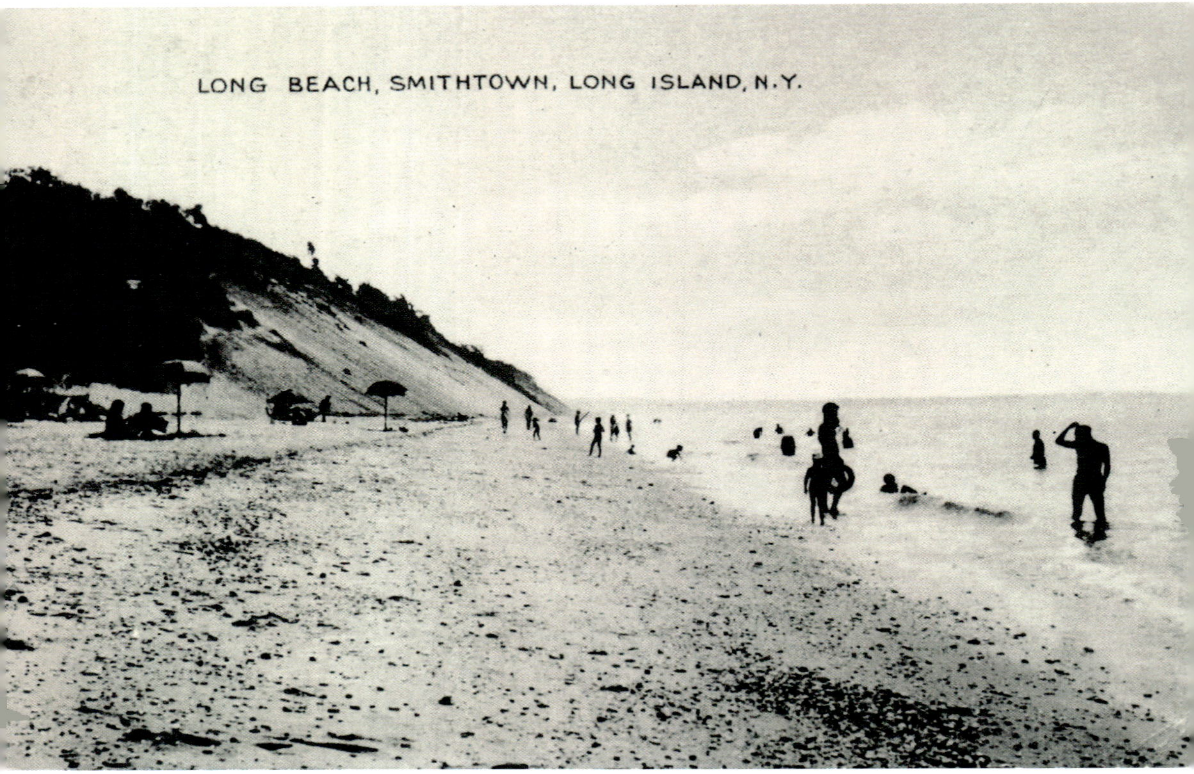

Long Beach is the designation of both an enormous, scenic peninsula that faces Smithtown Bay (part of the Long Island Sound) and a smaller town-run beach therein that became a public park in 1907. The land's beauty and fragility was recognized in colonial times. A 1747 town act prevented livestock from trampling over this enormous span of sandy land. Today, Long Beach Park contains a marina and boat ramp as well as facilities for swimming and fishing.

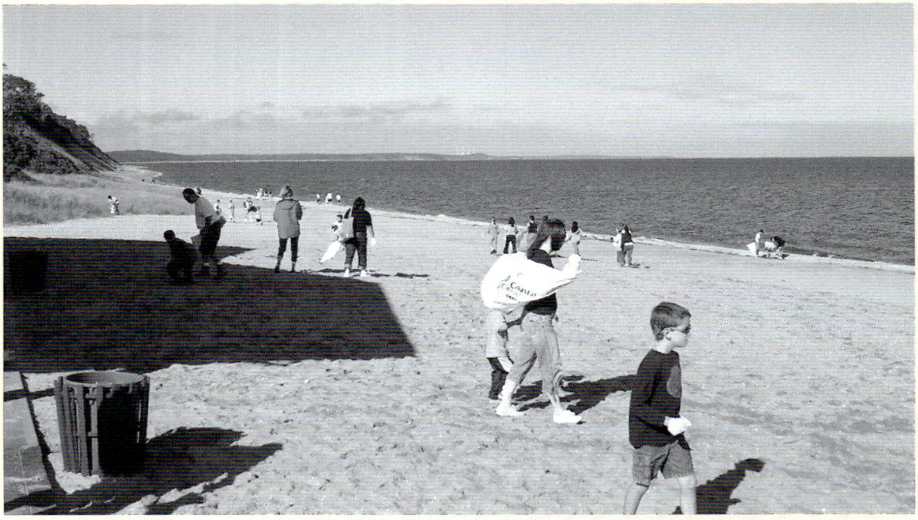

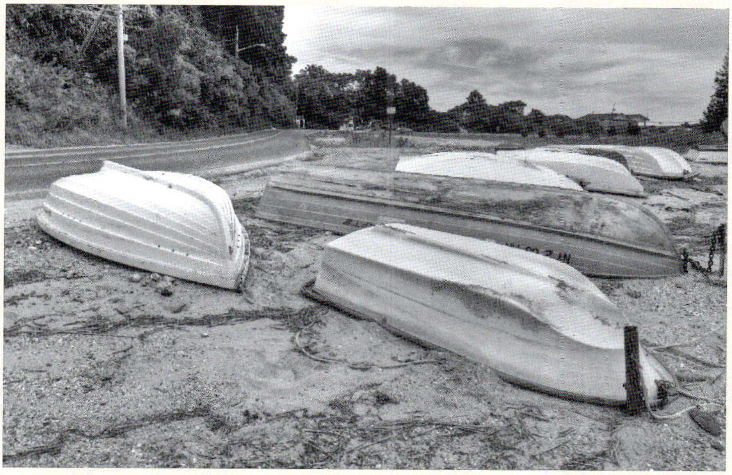

The Plank Road at Long Beach in Nissequogue was built in 1925. Tired of cars getting stranded in the sand, the Smithtown Outing and Beach Club wanted the Town of Smithtown to build a 2,300-foot plank road. The town board agreed to build the road after the club agreed to pay for its construction. The Thompson sisters were photographed in this 1930s picture walking along the plank road. Today, an asphalt roadway has replaced the original plank road. (Historic photograph courtesy David Thompson.)

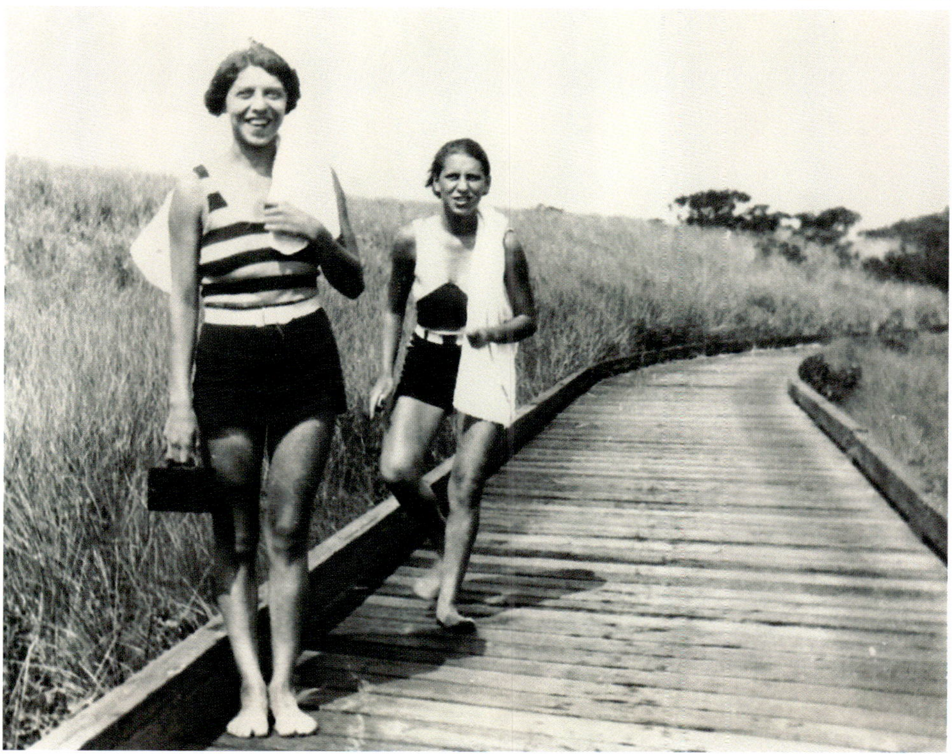

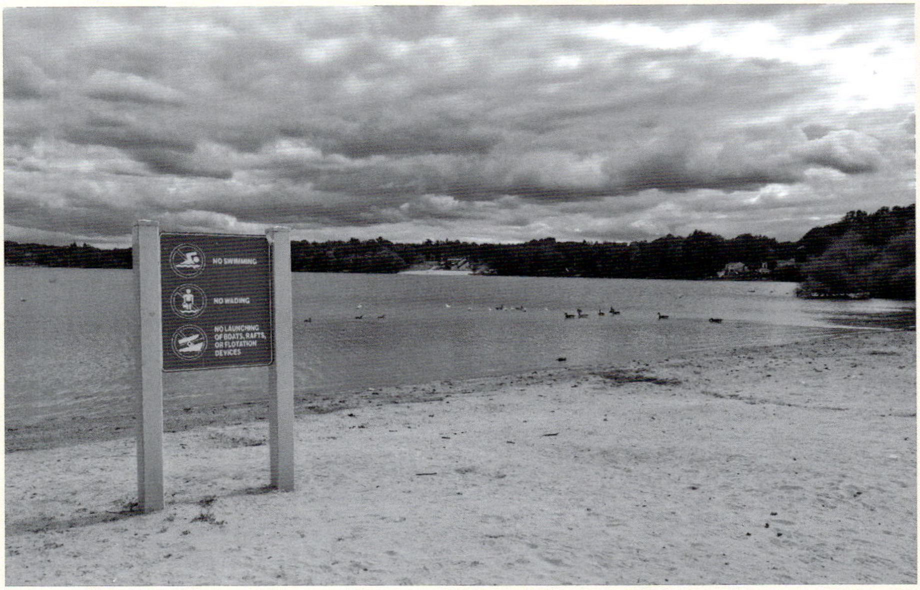

One mile in diameter, Lake Ronkonkoma covers portions of three townships—Smithtown, Brookhaven, and Islip. Historically, the lake beckoned to New York City tourists, especially during the early automotive years of the 1920s and 1930s. In the Nesconset-Smithtown portion of the lake, waterside entertainment flourished, and visitors often stayed in surrounding rented rooms, cottages, and tents. Unfortunately, due to pollution from storm water runoff contaminants, the lake is no longer safe for swimming.

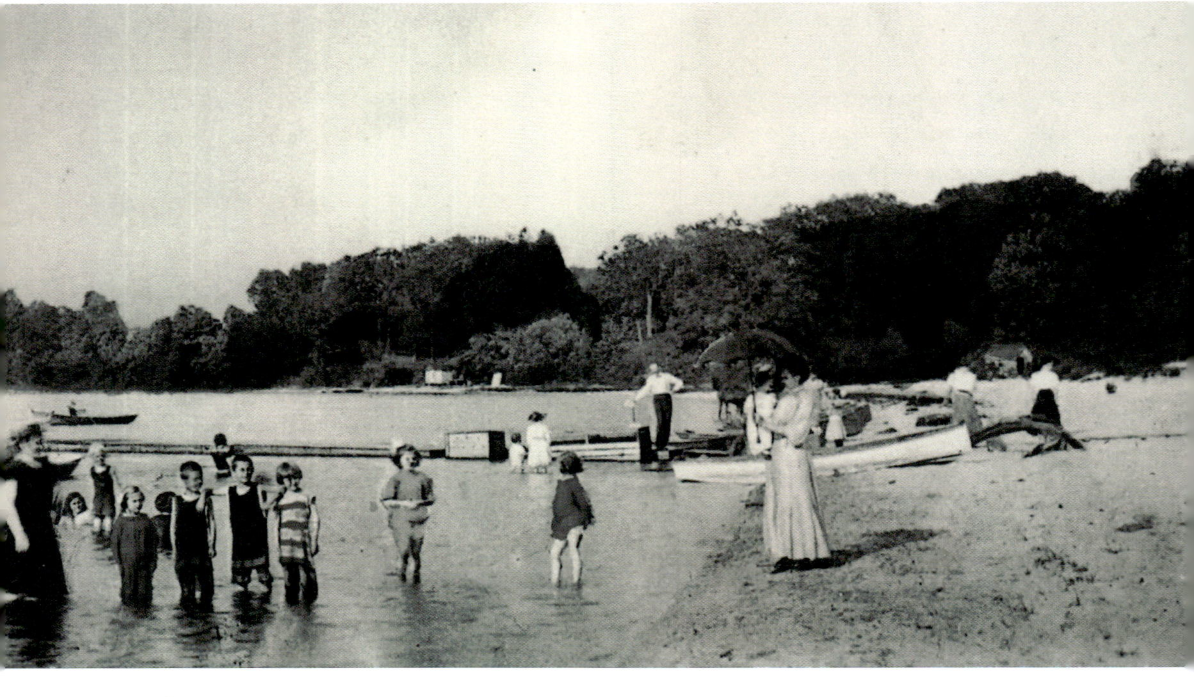

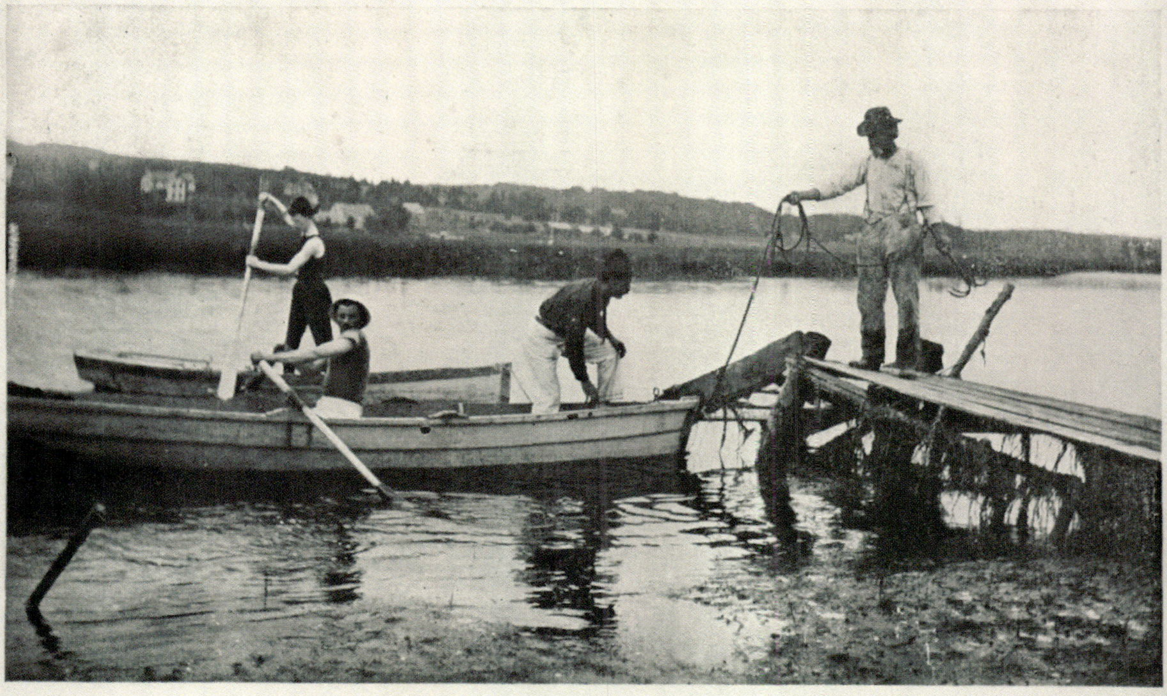

No. 17—Casting Off, Kings Park, L. I. T. J. MCCARTHY

Located at the northern end of Old Dock Road in Kings Park, Cornish's Dock (as it was once known) was a crucial hub of shipping activity during much of the 19th century. With the Long Island Railroad's (LIRR) arrival in 1872, however, the Nissequogue River and Long Island Sound soon fell out of favor as the primary avenue for transporting goods to and from the area. As the commercial shipping industry faded, the waterway's docks became increasingly utilized for recreational purposes.

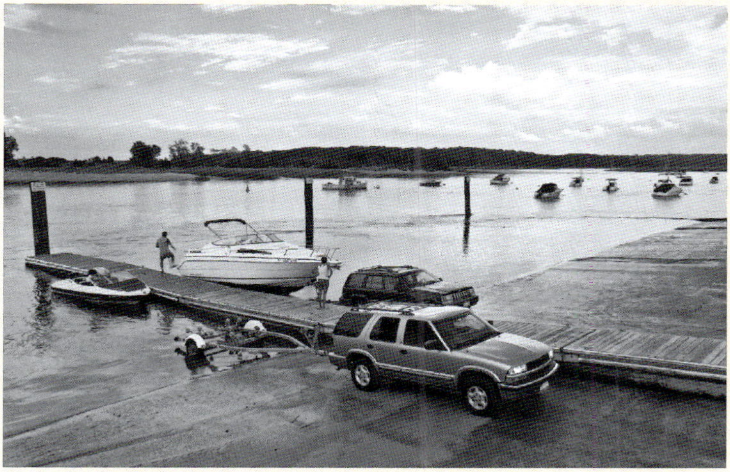

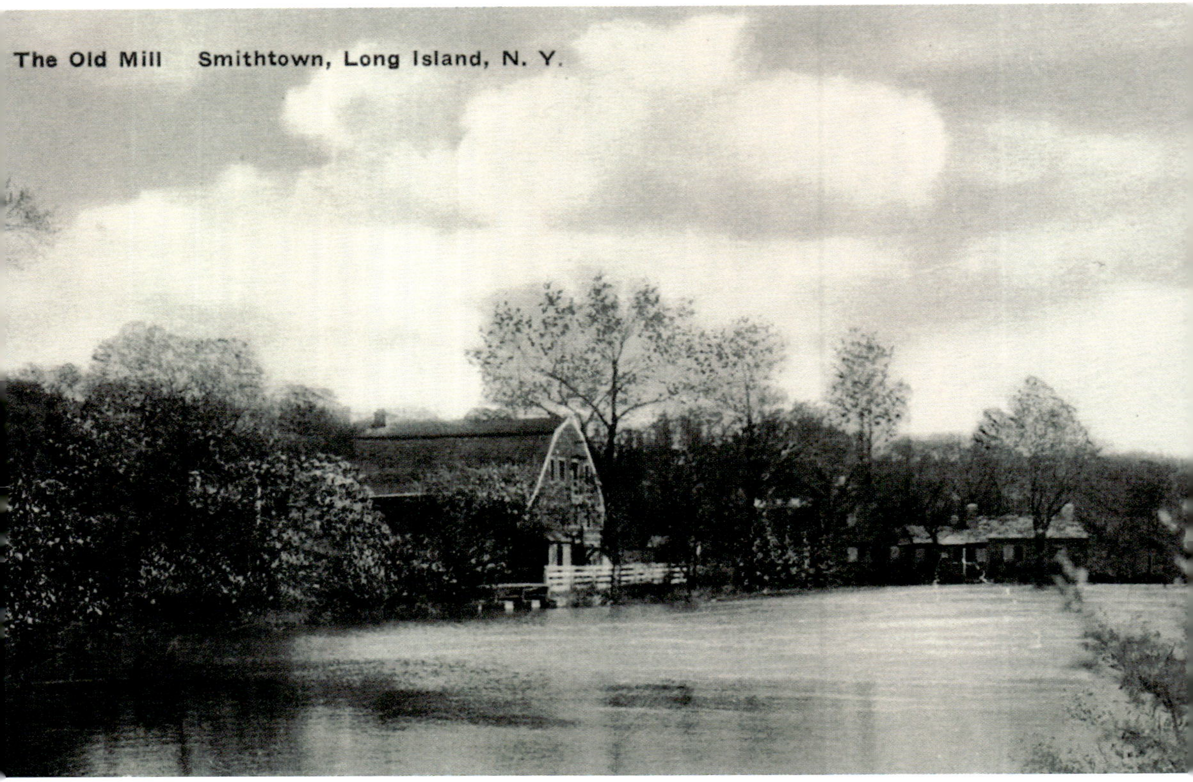

The dam across the Nissequogue River was built some time around 1725, and the gristmill and miller's house were built shortly thereafter. The only road through Head of the River ran across the dam, up Mill Dam Road, and then up New Mill Road into Smithtown Branch. Hidden behind the overgrowth of trees along the dam are the original buildings that make up the community of Head of the River, one of the best-preserved historic areas in Smithtown.

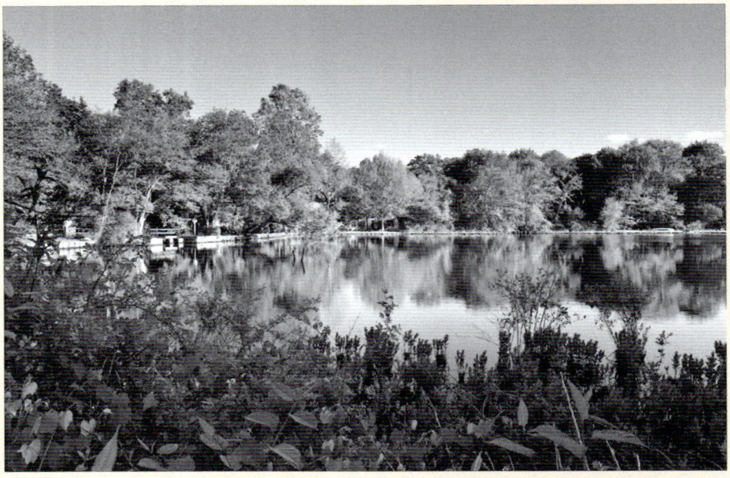

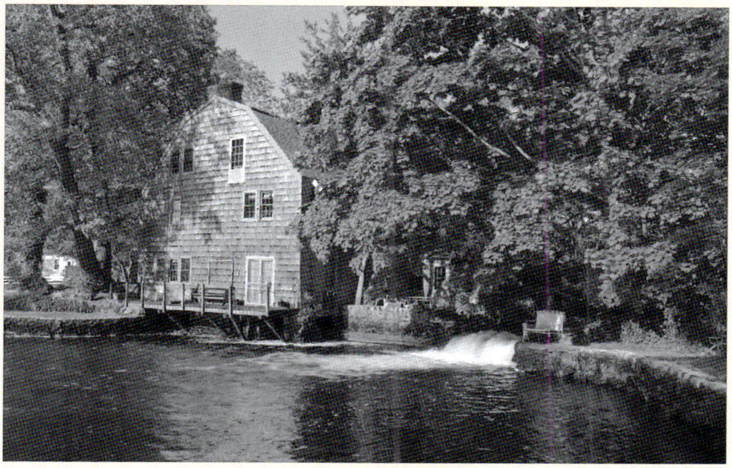

Built by Daniel Bates and Amos Willets some time after 1725, this gristmill was eventually sold to the Phillips family, who operated it as part of the Phillips Mills complex until 1882. Seen here around 1910, the mill was in operation until it was abandoned in 1909. In 1927, the White family purchased the site and converted it into a summer guesthouse. In 1958, Dr. Herbert Luther acquired the building and turned it into the year-round residence it remains today.

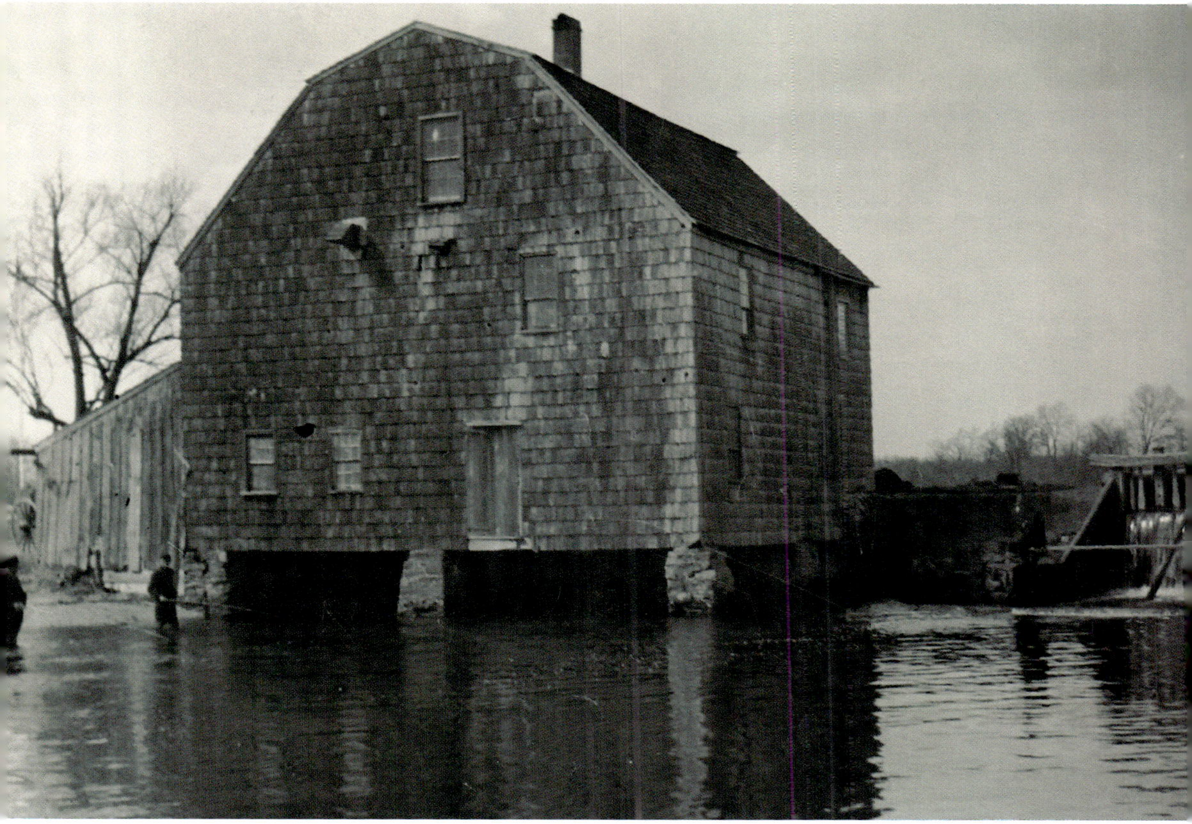

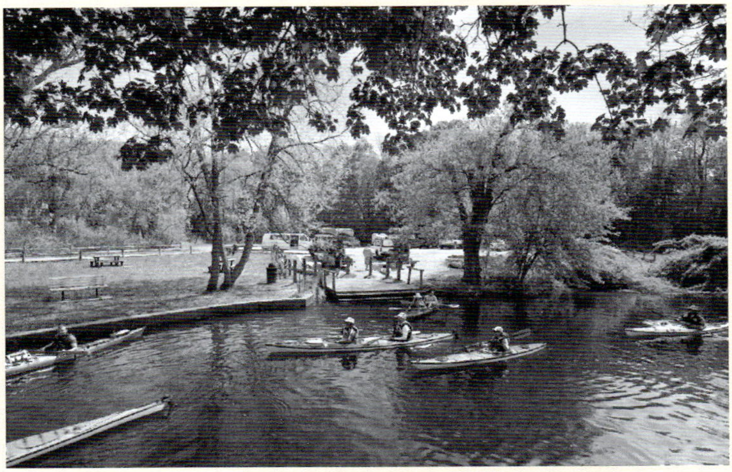

Popular with sportsmen from Brooklyn and New York, the Riverside Inn from the postcard view was built by the Loper brothers for proprietor William N. Spurge in 1901. Gov. Alfred E. Smith and New York City mayor Jimmy Walker enjoyed staying there in the 1920s. The inn later became a popular restaurant, Frank Friede's Riverside Inn, known for its German dishes until it was destroyed by fire in 1981. Today, this spot is county parkland with a canoe launch.

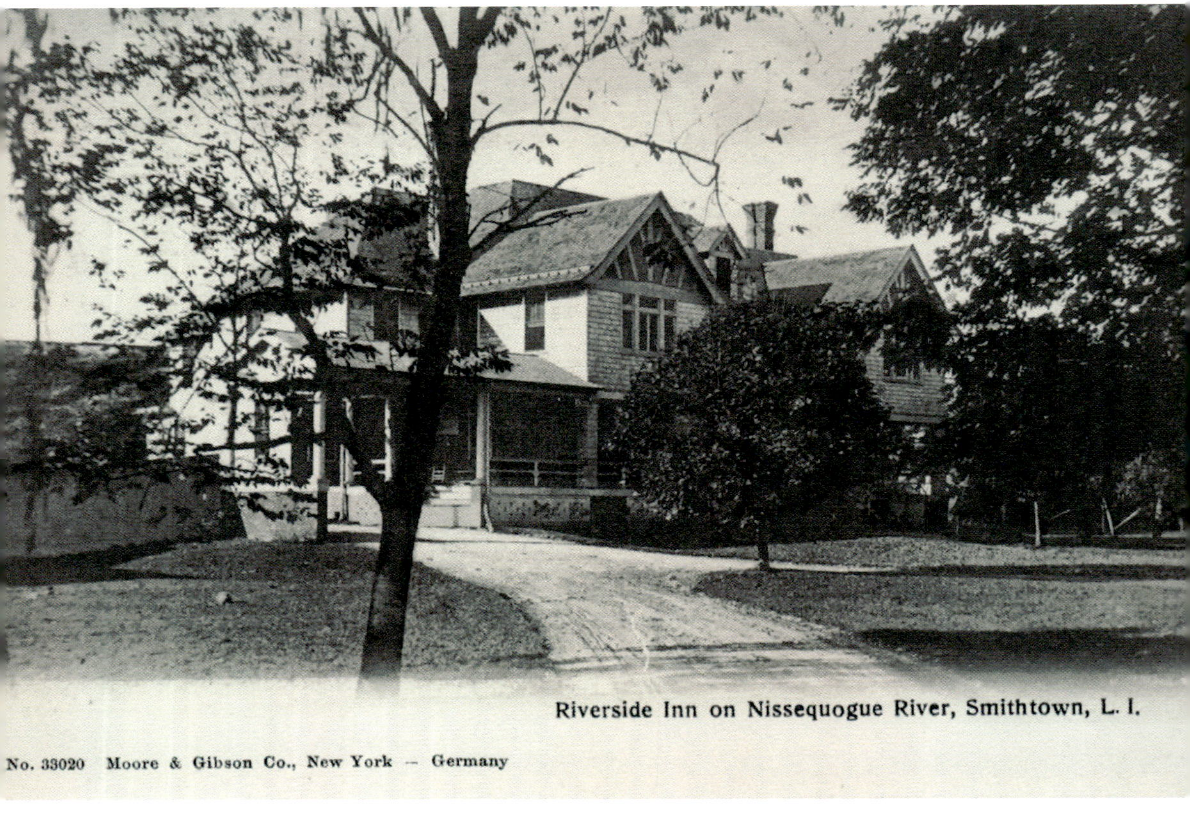

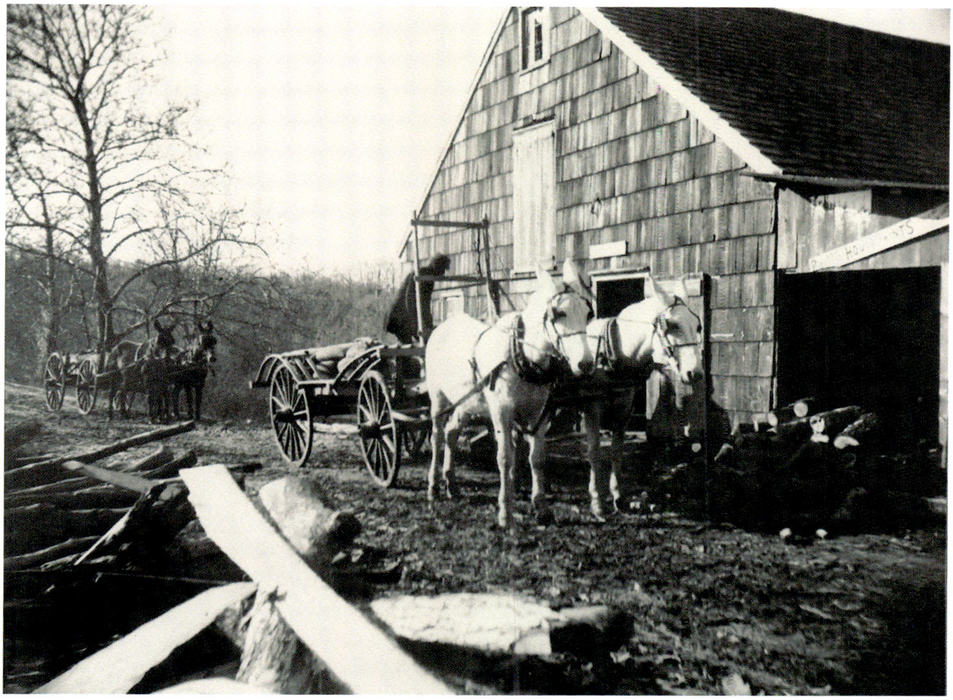

In 1798, an agreement reached by Caleb Smith II, Joshua Smith II, and Isaac Blydenburgh led to the construction of a new dam on the northwest branch of the Nissequogue River. This damming effort created a millpond, called Stump Pond because of the number of submerged tree stumps it contained; in 1799, a new gristmill and sawmill were erected on the site. In the photograph, a wagonload of grain is being unloaded at the gristmill.

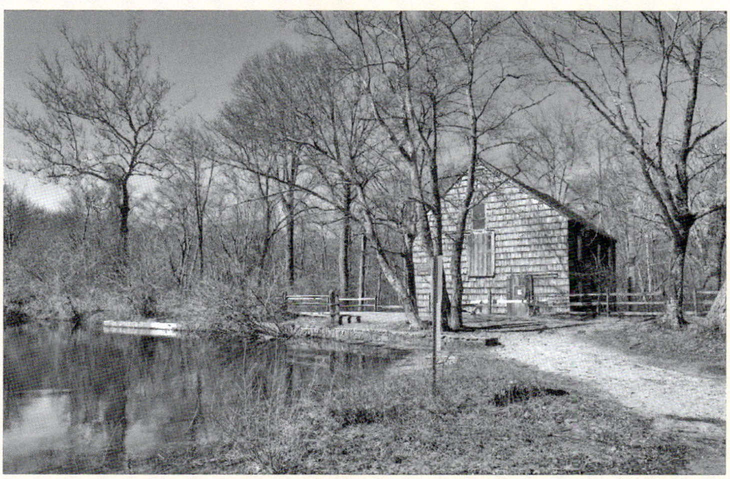

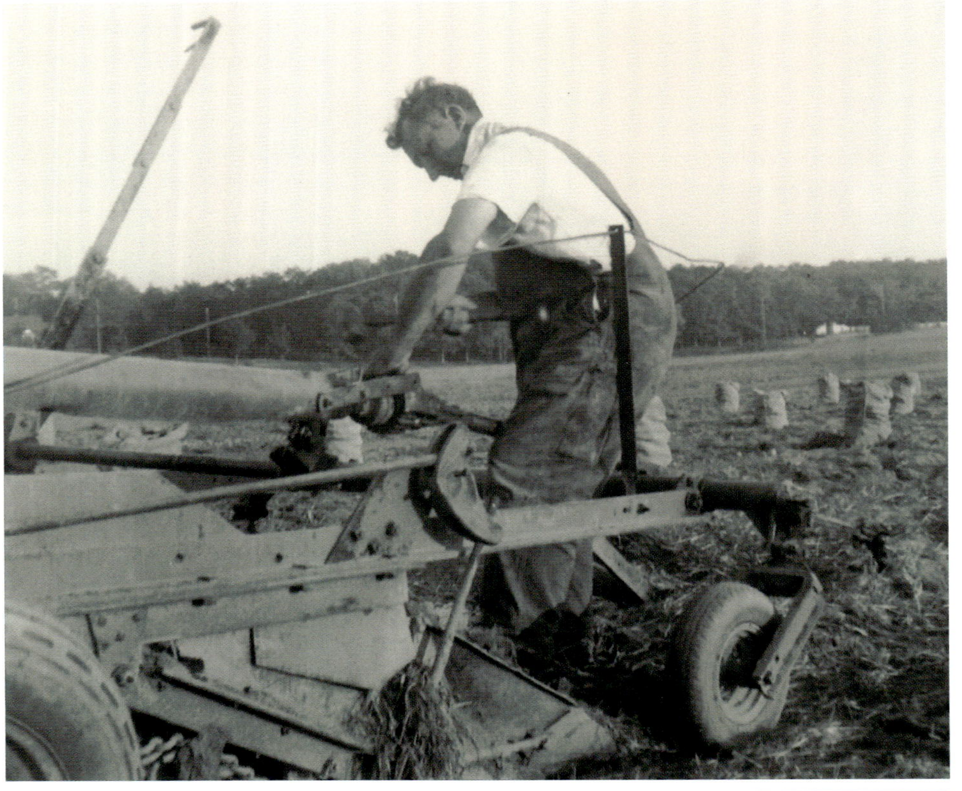

Joseph Borello was a potato farmer in Plainview until the golden nematode got into his fields, forcing him to sell his farm and relocate further east on Long Island. In 1950, he purchased a 96-acre farm on Edgewood Avenue in Smithtown. He planted potatoes and cabbage on his land, and this photograph, taken in 1955, captures Joe repairing a potato combine in his fields, the same fields where his son-in-law Steve Gallagher is now growing grapes at Whisper's Vineyard. (Historic photograph courtesy Steve Gallagher.)

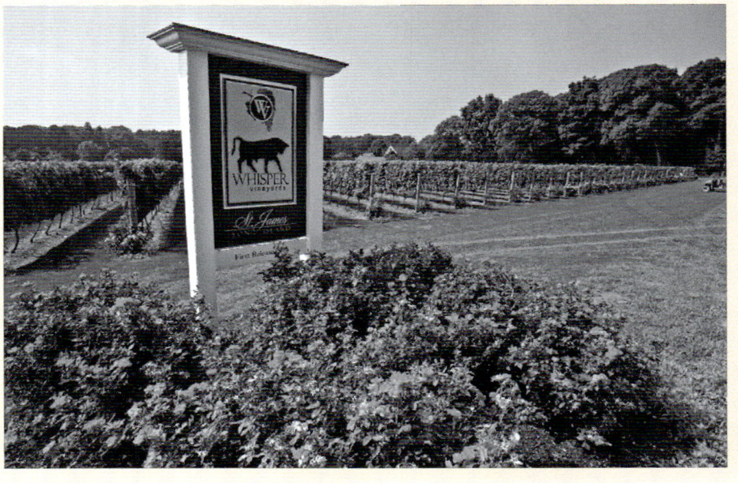

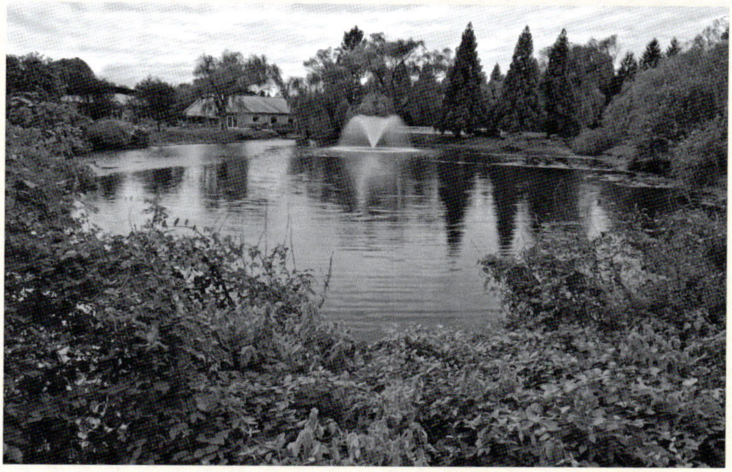

Flowerfield, located on the southeast corner of the intersection of Mills Pond and North Country Roads in St. James, started out as the country home of Childs' Famous Flowers. Flower bulbs were planted here and harvested for sale in New York City markets. During World War II, potatoes replaced flowers to support the war effort. Today, a catering facility leases part of the property, and Stony Brook University has acquired much of the remaining open land. (Historic photograph courtesy Lee Corbari.)

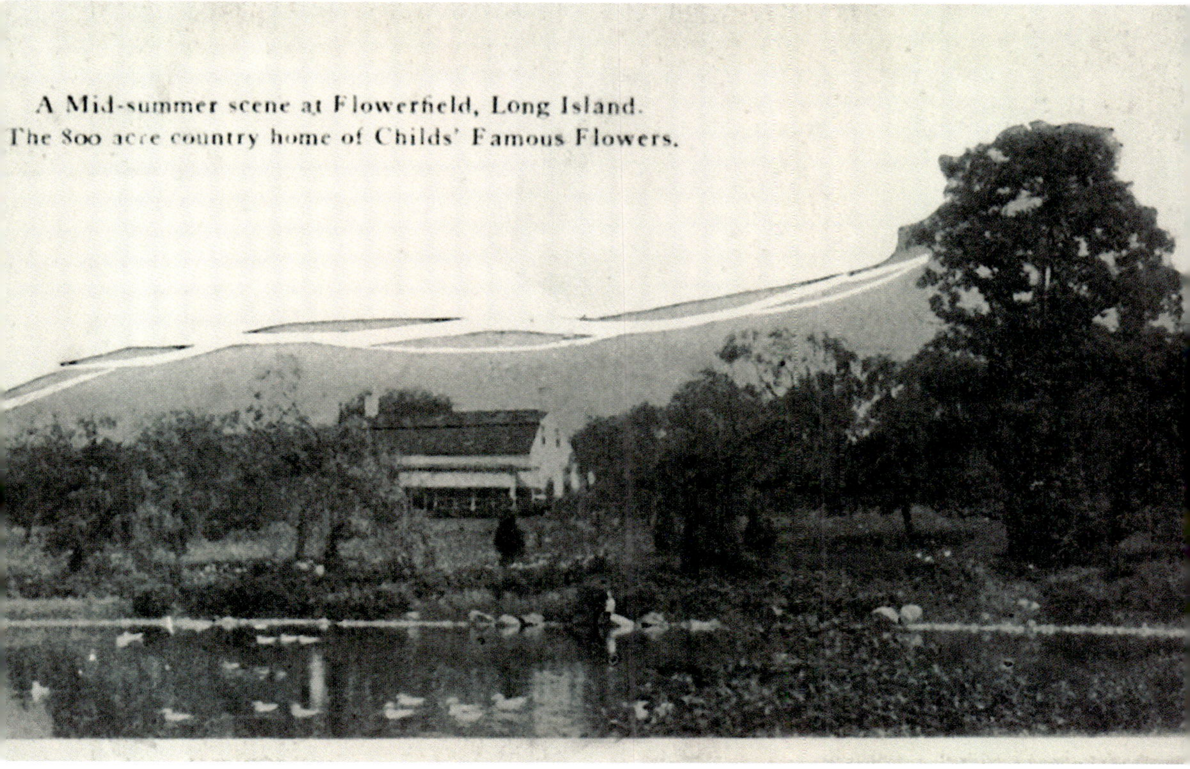

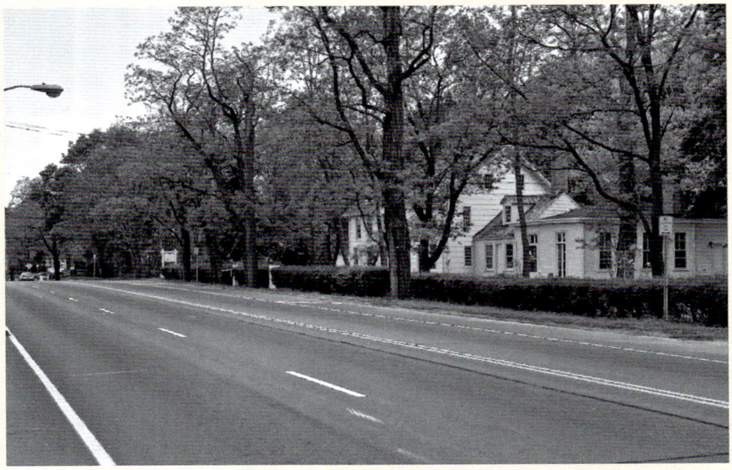

While the public's preservation focus tends to revolve around historic buildings, natural landscape features are often even more vulnerable. The historic photograph on this page exhibits the tall shipmast locust trees—a rare species that was especially valued for shipbuilding and fence posts—that were initially planted by Judge J. Lawrence Smith in the 1850s. Most of these trees in the Village of the Branch fell as victim to a road-widening project in the 1980s.

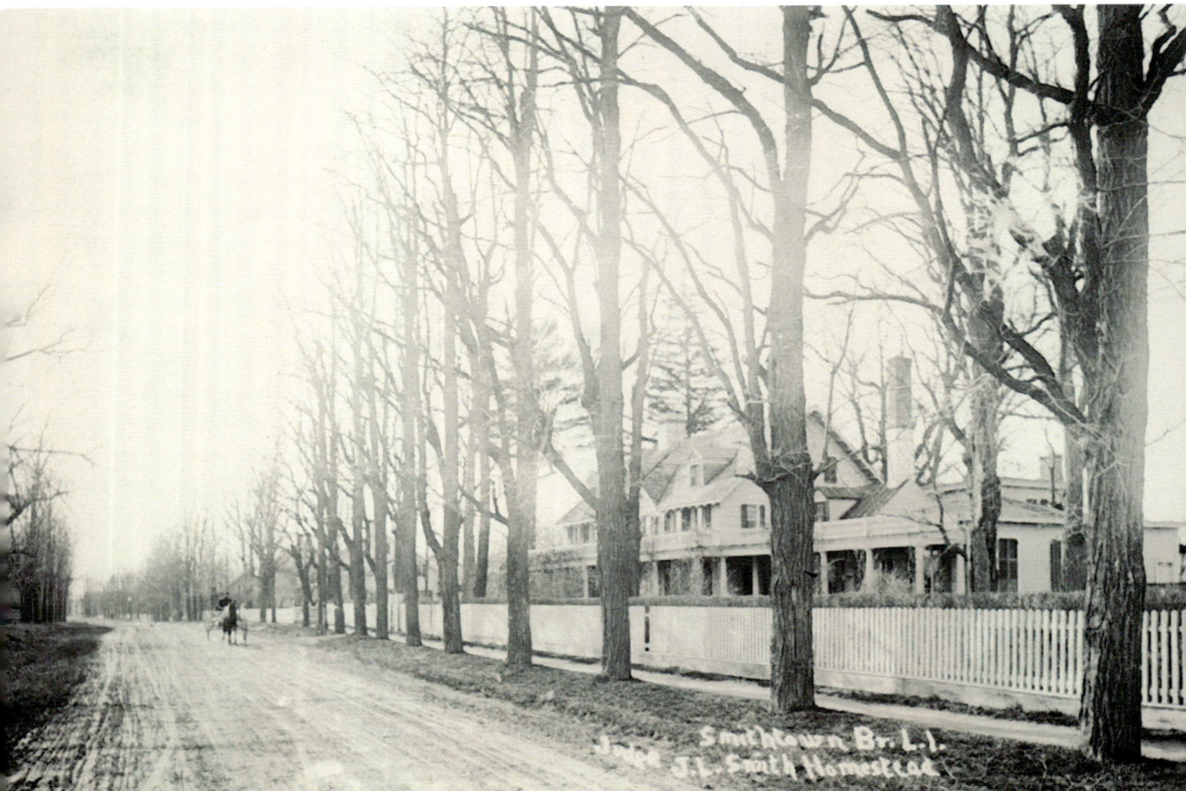

CHAPTER 3

PRAYER AND STUDY

RELIGIOUS CENTERS AND SCHOOLS

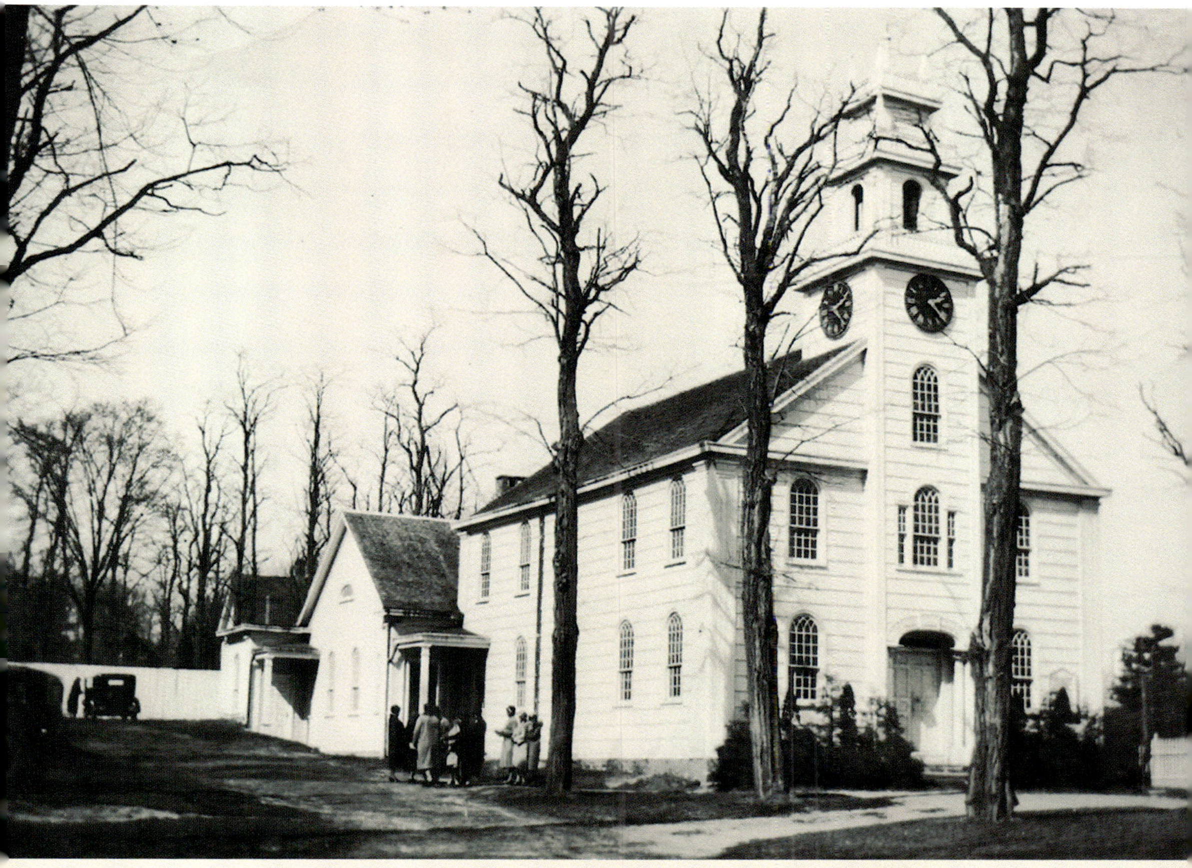

Though the current building was constructed in 1827, the First Presbyterian Church of Smithtown has presided over the junction of Route 25, North Country Road, and River Road since it moved from a location closer to the mouth of the Nissequogue River in 1750. Later additions to the church include the narthex (1898), parish hall (1950), and education wing (1963).

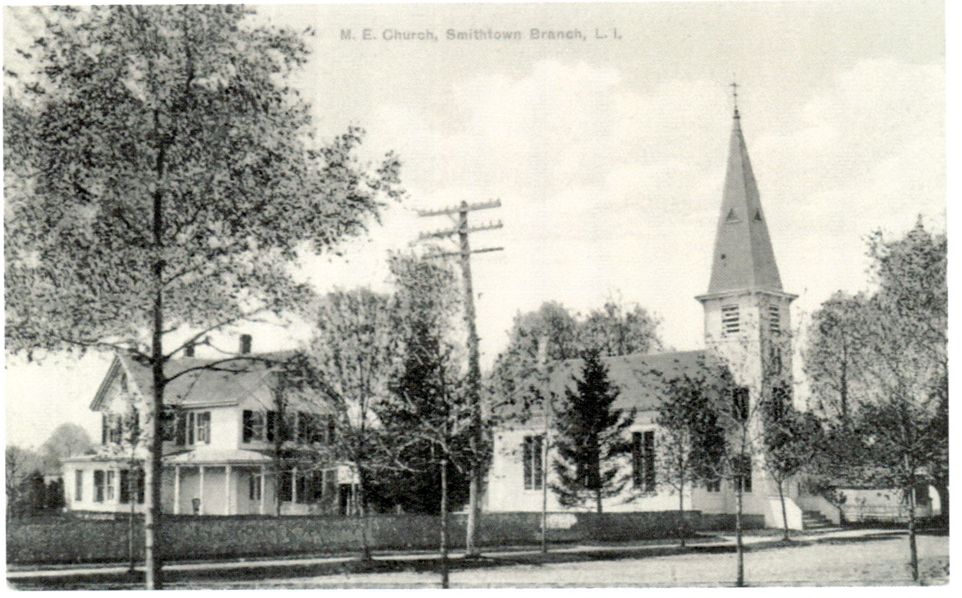

The old Methodist church on Main Street, with its picturesque six-sided bell tower (added in the 1930s), was razed in 1962. It had been moved from its original location on the west side of Judge's Lane to this site in 1885. Smithtown's new Methodist church was built due east of the first spot, on Middle Country Road. The new church incorporated a number of elements from the old building: the bell, stained-glass windows, lectern and pews. (Historic photograph courtesy Smithtown Library, Maggie Land Blanck Collection.)

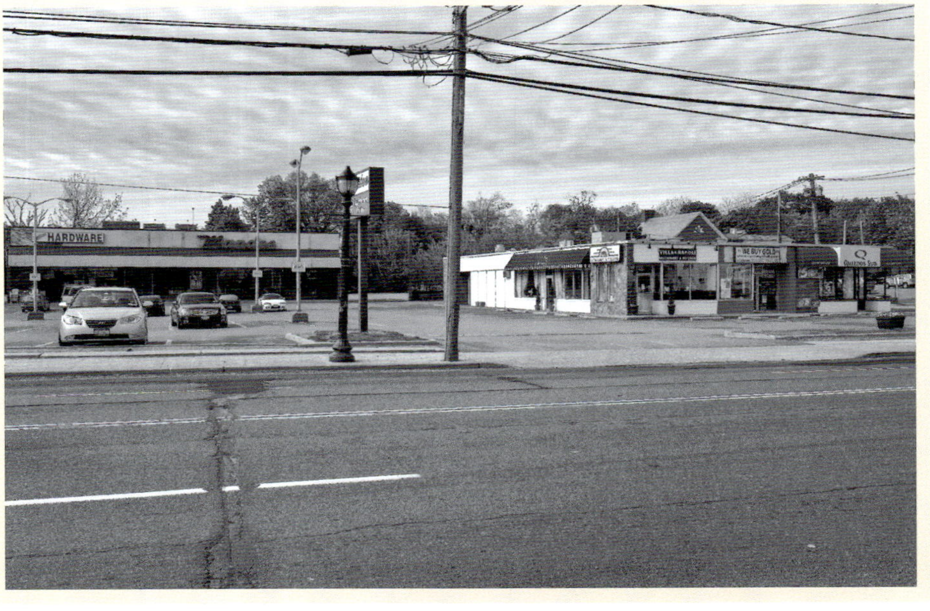

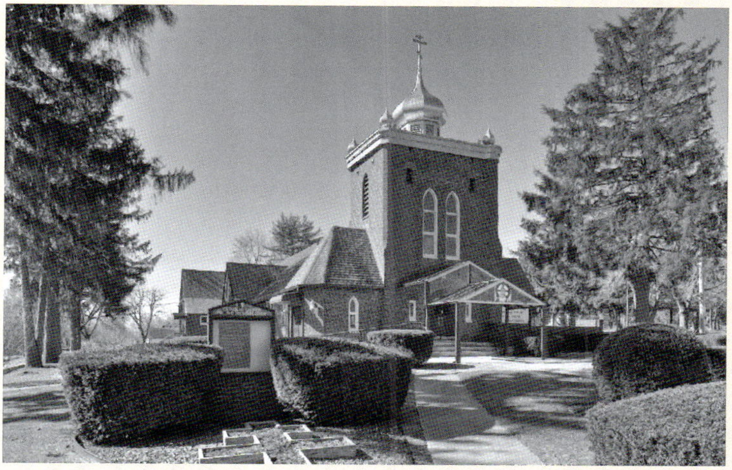

Smithtown's earliest Catholic church was built in the 1840s. This particular church was erected in 1927 and was home to St. Patrick's Roman Catholic parish for nearly 40 years. Smithtown's Byzantine Catholic community has called this structure, now known as Resurrection Byzantine Catholic Church, home since 1967. Its striking onion domes, a typical feature of Byzantine architecture, were added to the church in 1979.

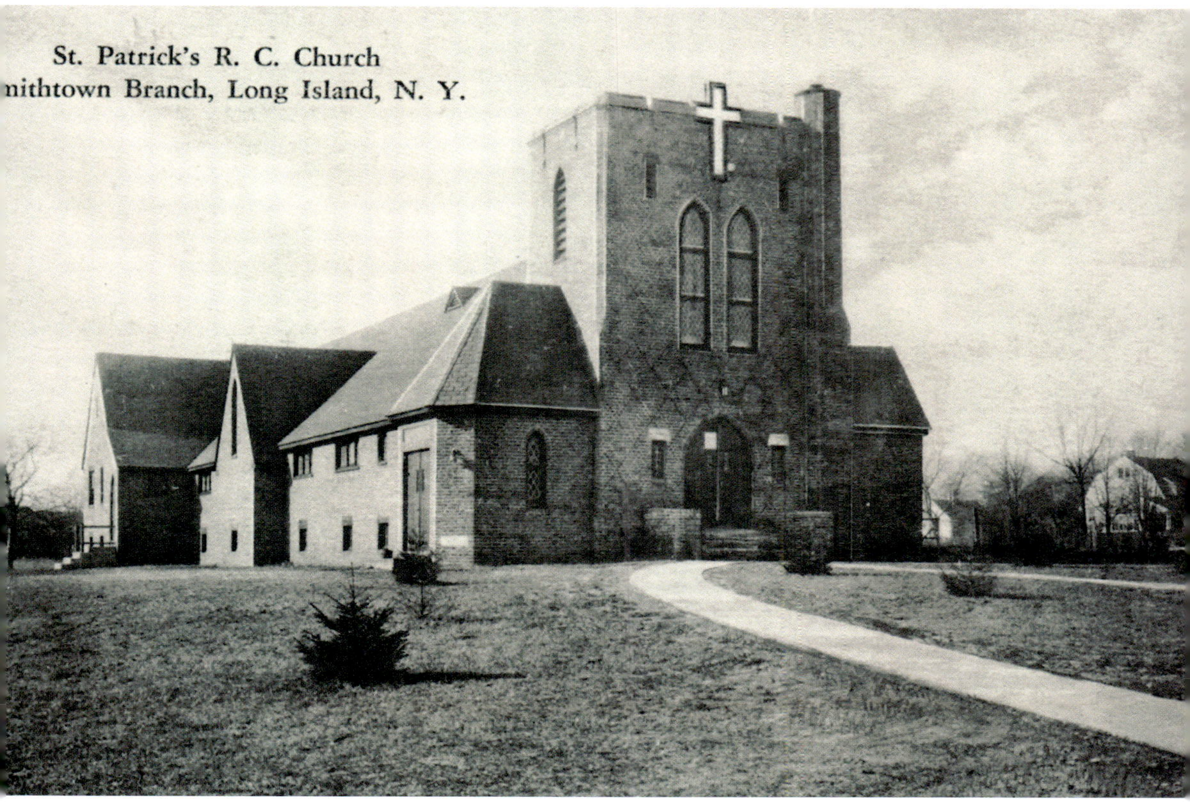

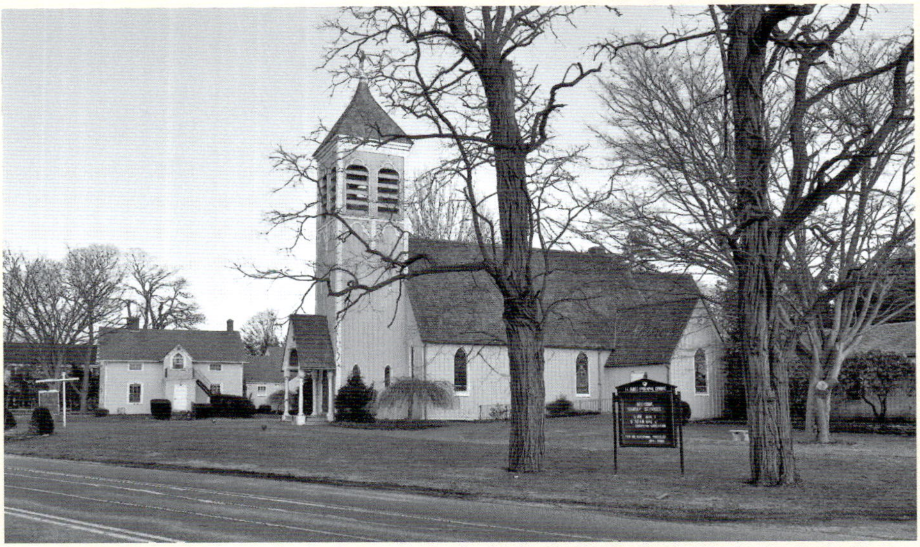

The St. James Episcopal Church, located at 490 North Country Road, was built in 1854 by local Episcopalians desiring a house of worship closer to home than their former churches in Setauket and Islip. In his 1882 account *The History of Smithtown*, original churchwarden John Lawrence Smith wrote that the church was named St. James "in compliment to James Clinch of New York, through whose instrumentality and liberality the church was organized and, in its infancy, mainly supported."

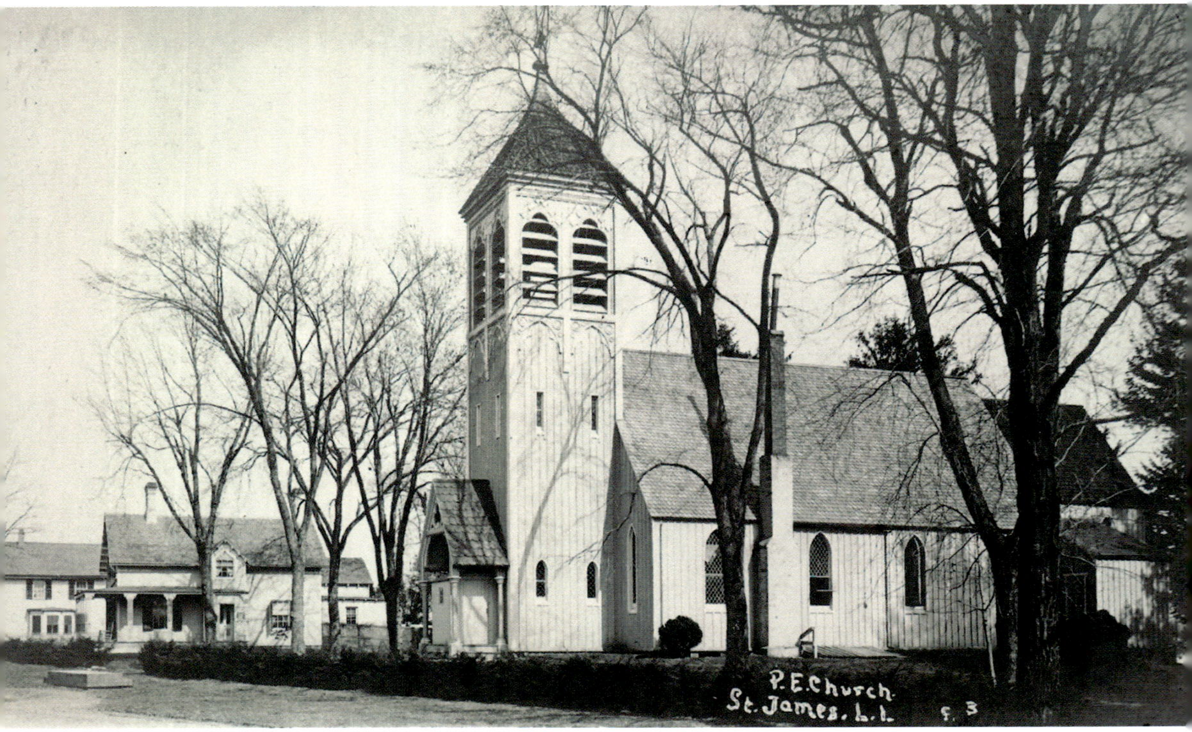

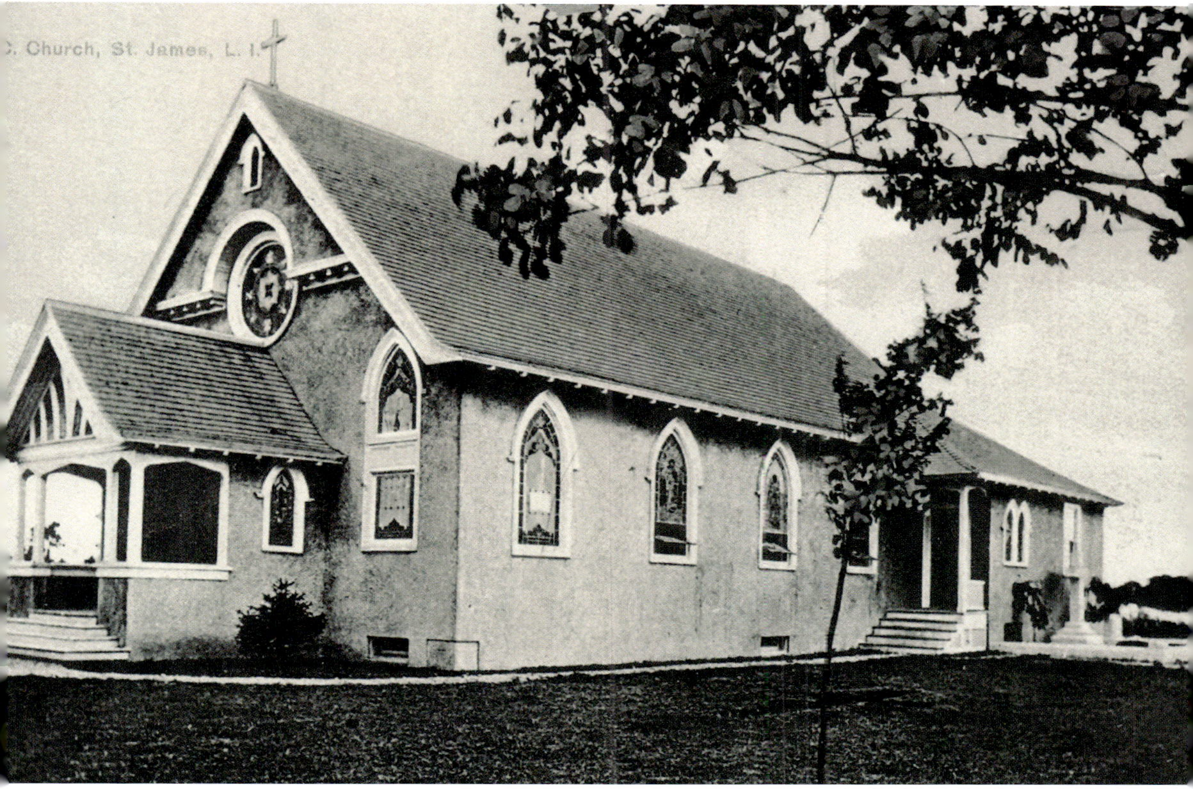

The St. Philip and St. James Roman Catholic Church parish was founded when a young priest named Father William J. Duhigg began celebrating mass in an old schoolhouse in St. James's Actors' Colony in 1907. Enlisting his friends from Catholic churches in Brooklyn, Father Duhigg raised the money to build a Catholic church in St. James. Dedicated on September 5, 1909, the original St. Philip and St. James Church served the community until the current church building was constructed in 1962.

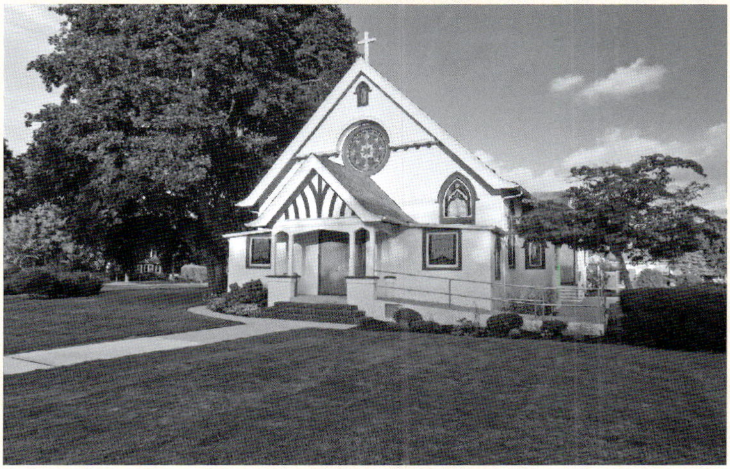

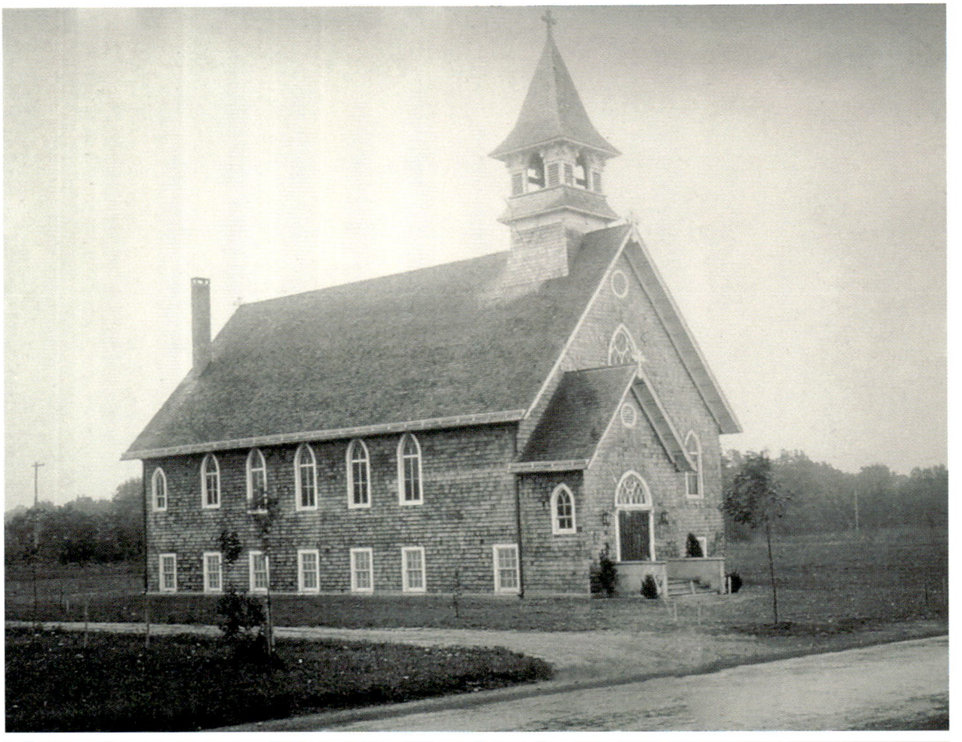

When the St. James Lutheran Church was built on Woodlawn Avenue in 1928, it was surrounded by open land. In the 1920s, a number of Norwegian, Swedish, and German immigrants made their way to St. James and purchased building lots in St. James Park, a housing development south of the LIRR tracks with a grid of intersecting streets and avenues. They brought their Lutheran faith with them and in 1928 built a Lutheran church in the midst of their homes. (Historic photograph courtesy Carole Nelson.)

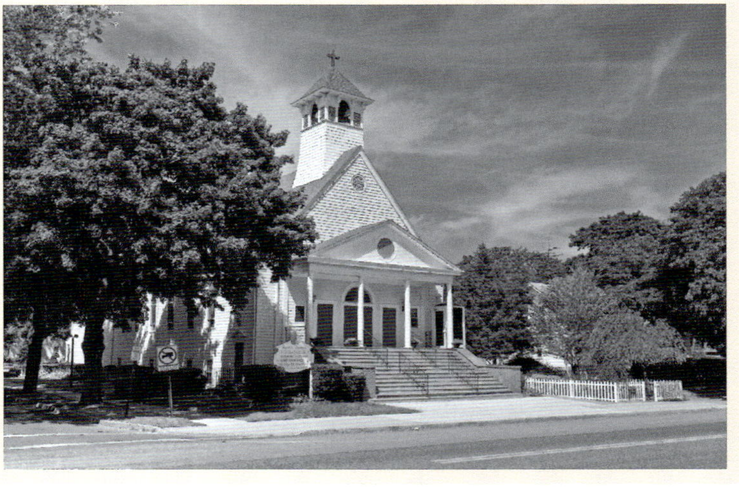

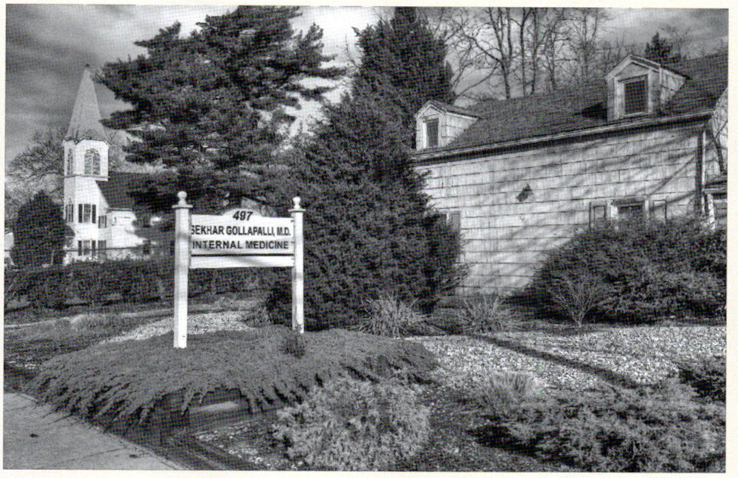

The Lawrence family was out for a sleigh ride when they stopped in front of the Cornish House to have this photograph taken in 1912. Built shortly after the Hauppauge United Methodist Church was erected on Town Line Road in 1806, the Cornish House is one of the oldest surviving homes near the church. While the church building looks largely the same today, the Cornish House has since been renovated and converted into a doctor's office.

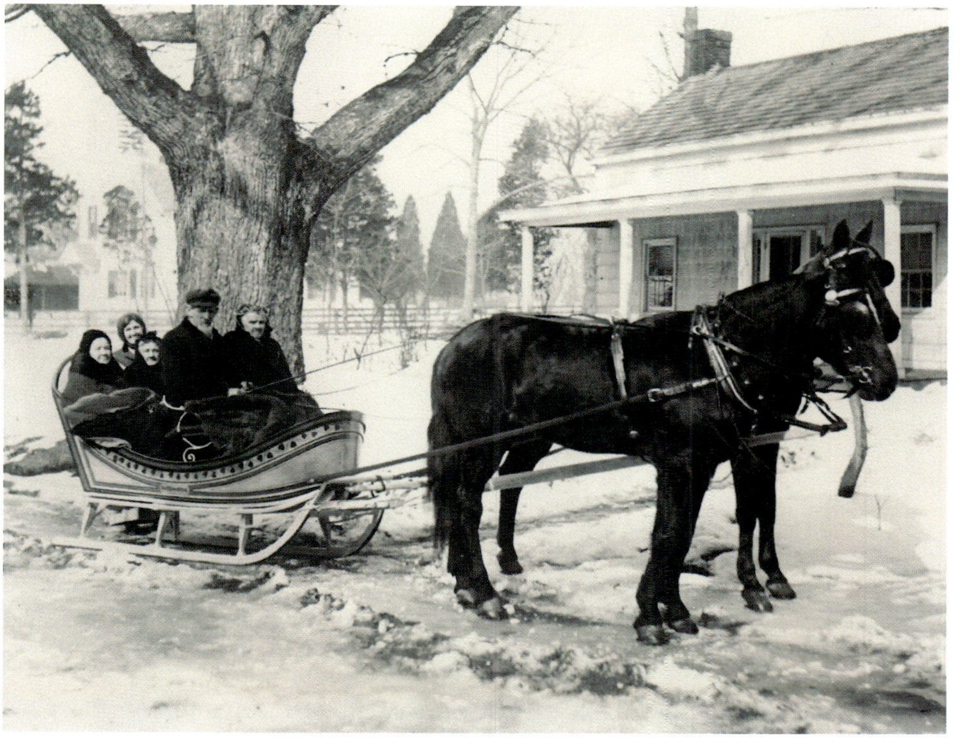

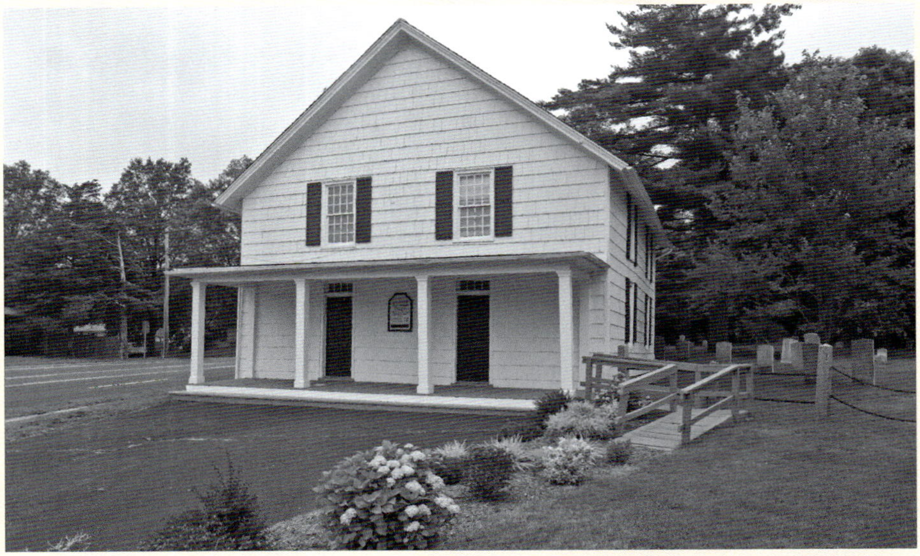

Just off of Townline Road, this is the oldest Methodist church building on Long Island, dating to 1789. An old cemetery sits adjacent to the structure. While the congregation expanded in the mid-20th century, the church leadership thankfully decided to preserve the original structure, even after building a new sanctuary next door. The older chapel is still used for several services annually by the Commack United Methodist congregation and every Sunday by the Long Island Korean United Methodist Church.

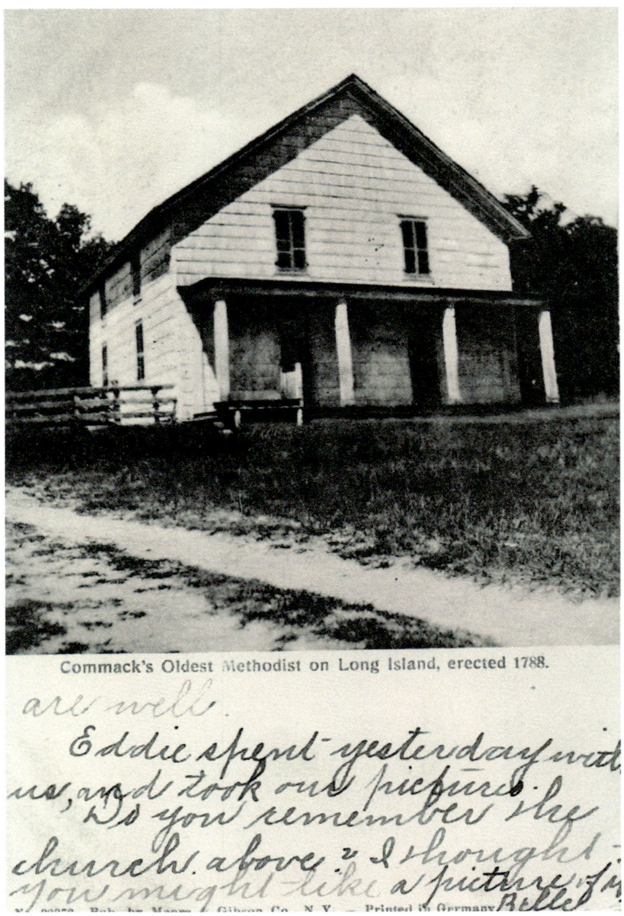

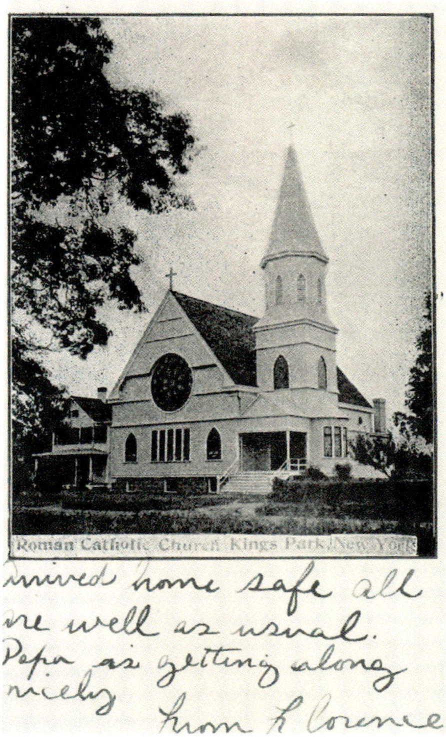

The Church of St. Joseph in Kings Park was built in 1899. The effort to raise funds to build a Catholic church in Kings Park was begun in 1894, and a total of $17,000 was raised to build the structure. The cornerstone was laid in 1898, and a year later, the church was dedicated. The wooden church building served the community until 1958, when the present brick Church of St. Joseph replaced it.

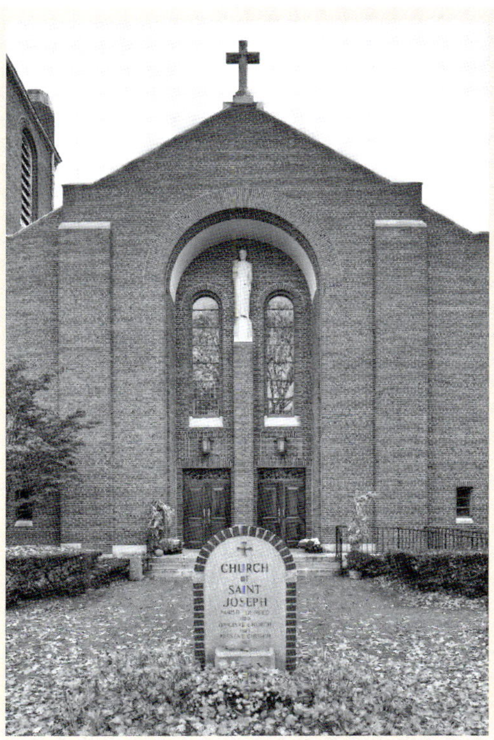

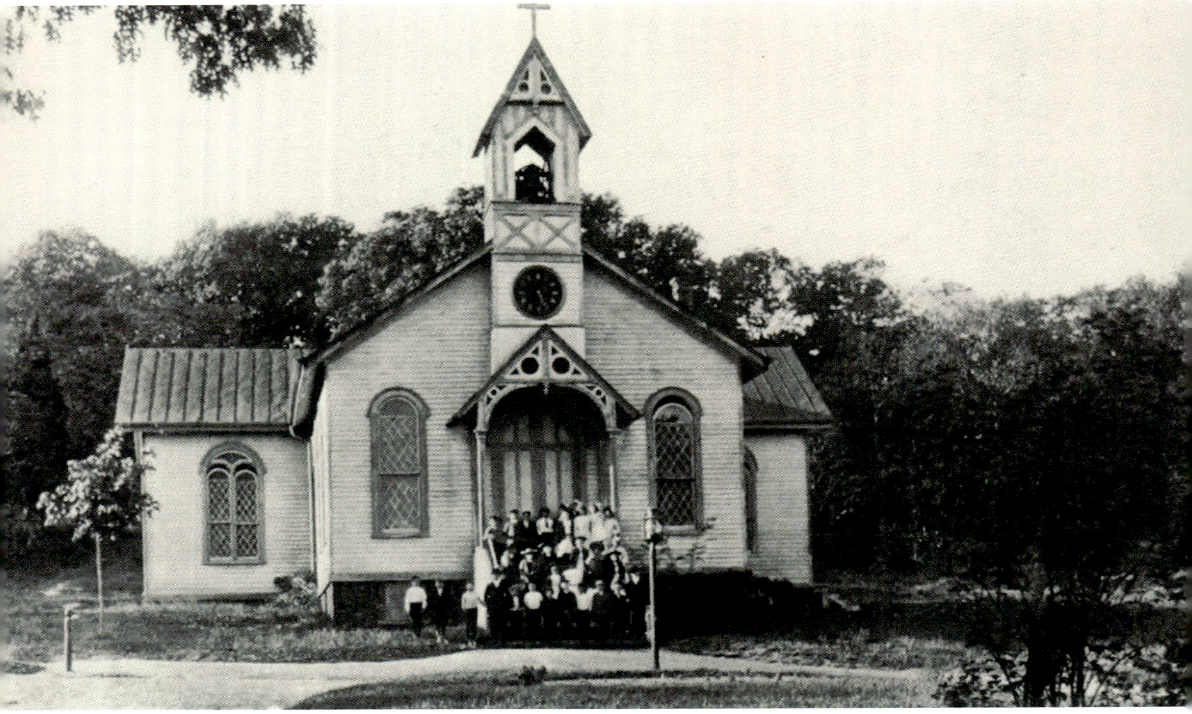

The Church of the Testimony of Jesus, the Society of St. Johnland's chapel, was built in 1869. This Episcopal chapel stood in the middle of the St. Johnland settlement, a constant reminder to those in the utopian community that they were the recipients of Christian charity. This chapel was destroyed in 1917 by a fire caused by a faulty furnace. At the end of World War I, the society built the brick chapel that occupies the site today.

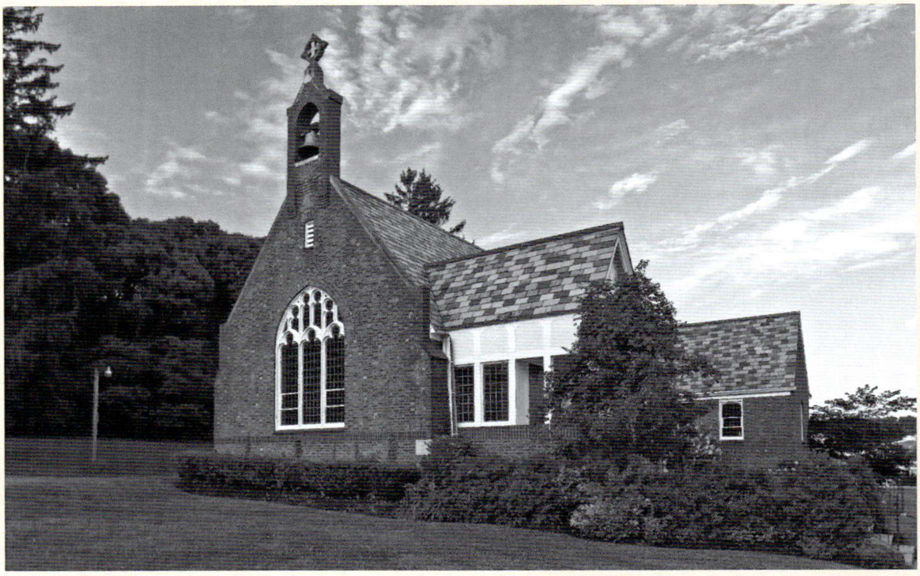

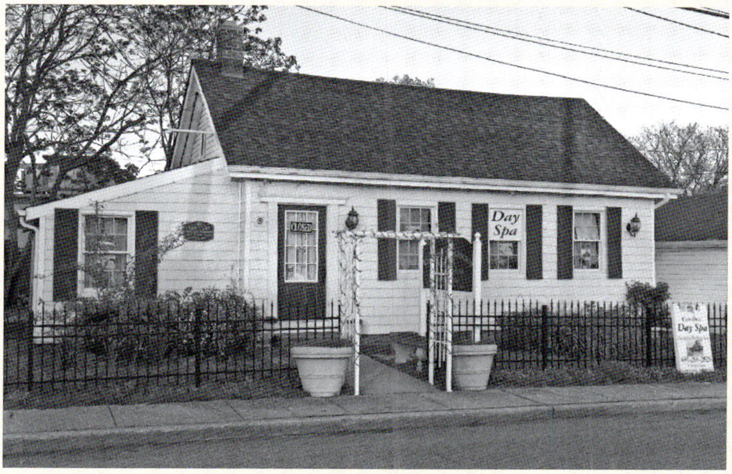

Opened as a private school in 1802, the first schoolhouse in Smithtown Branch once stood on the north side of Main Street, west of the Presbyterian church. In 1816, the one-room structure became a tax-supported common school in the Branch School District. It continued to serve the district until James Darling bought the building and relocated it to its present location on the east side of Singer Lane in 1868. The schoolhouse is now occupied by a day spa.

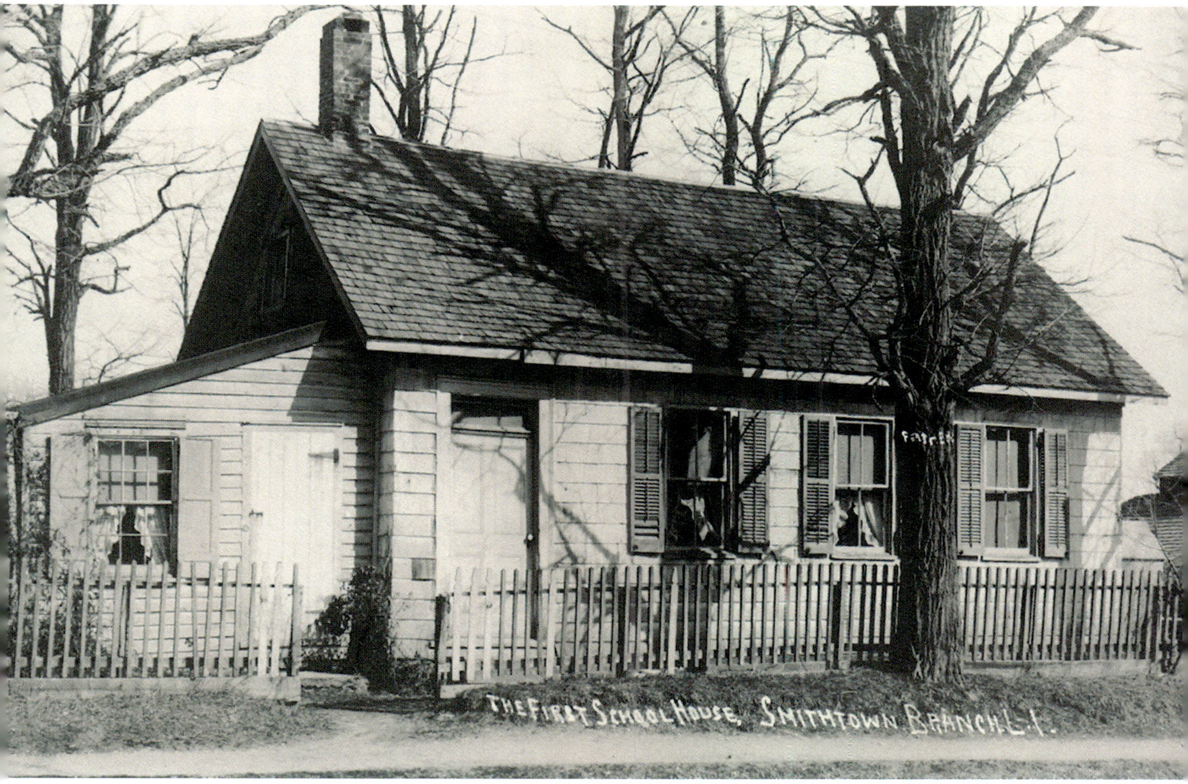

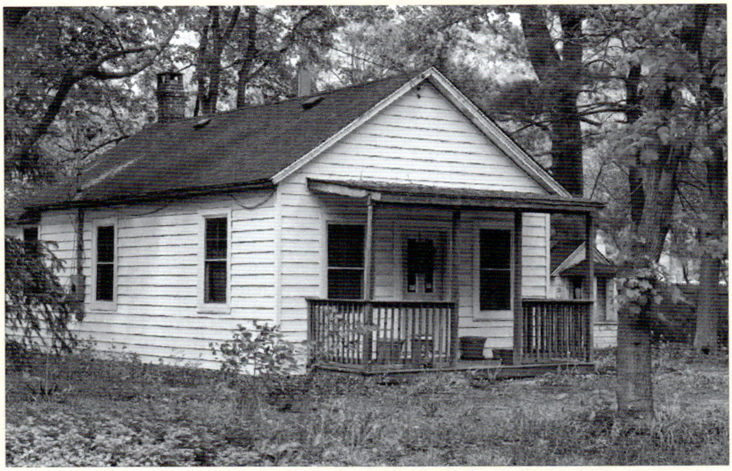

A tiny one-room schoolhouse for the Head of the River community until 1922, this building is on the north side of Meadow Road. It had an open front porch where children gathered before going inside to begin their lessons. Like many buildings in Smithtown, and though heavily remodeled, this structure was originally on a different site. It was built on the property of Ebenezer Blydenburgh, north of New Mill Road, and moved around 1880.

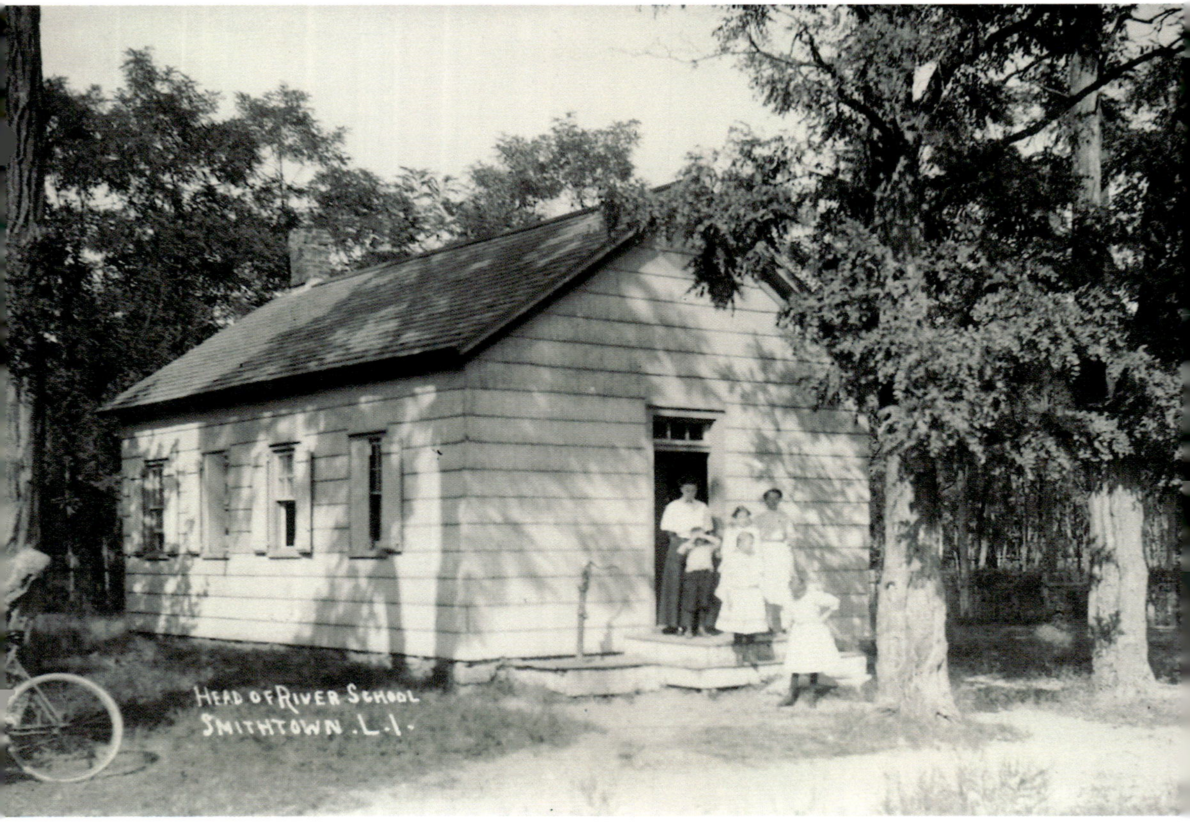

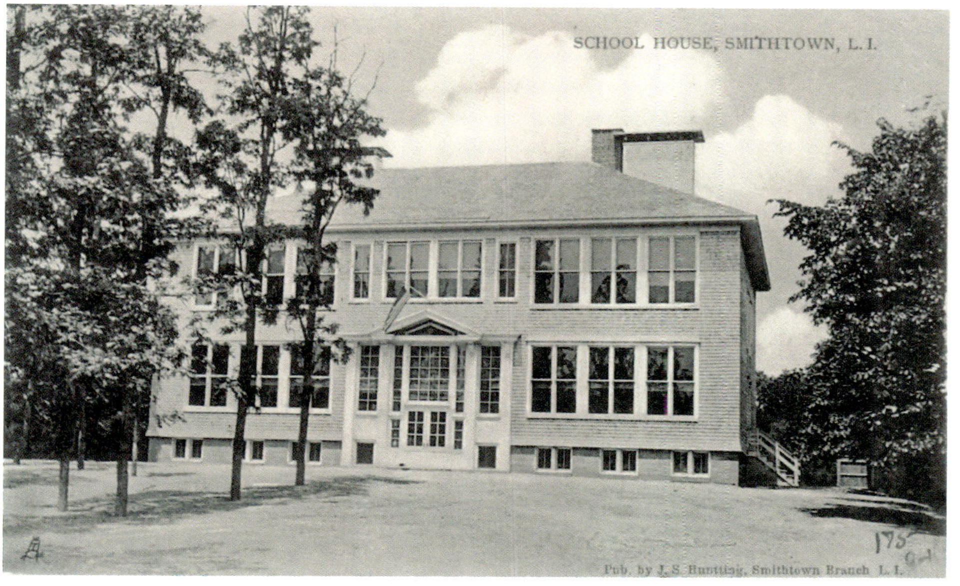

The Smithtown Branch School was erected in 1910 on the former site of the Academy. It was a two-story building that had heat and electricity but no inside toilets. When it opened, it served only grades one through nine, though a high school program was soon added. When the New York Avenue School was opened in 1925, this school was closed. During the Depression, the building was used as a welfare office. It was ultimately demolished in the 1950s. (Historic photograph courtesy Smithtown Library, Maggie Land Blanck Collection.)

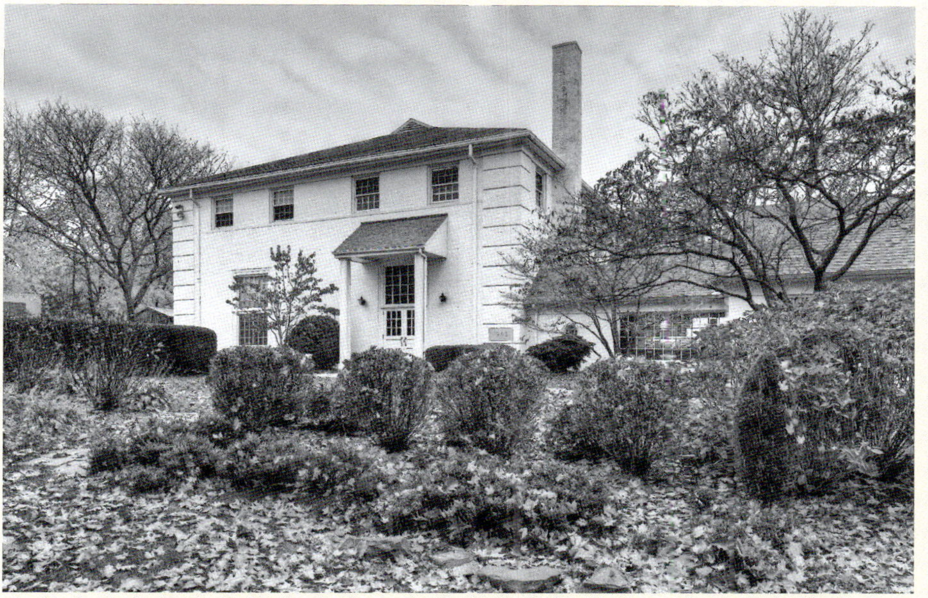

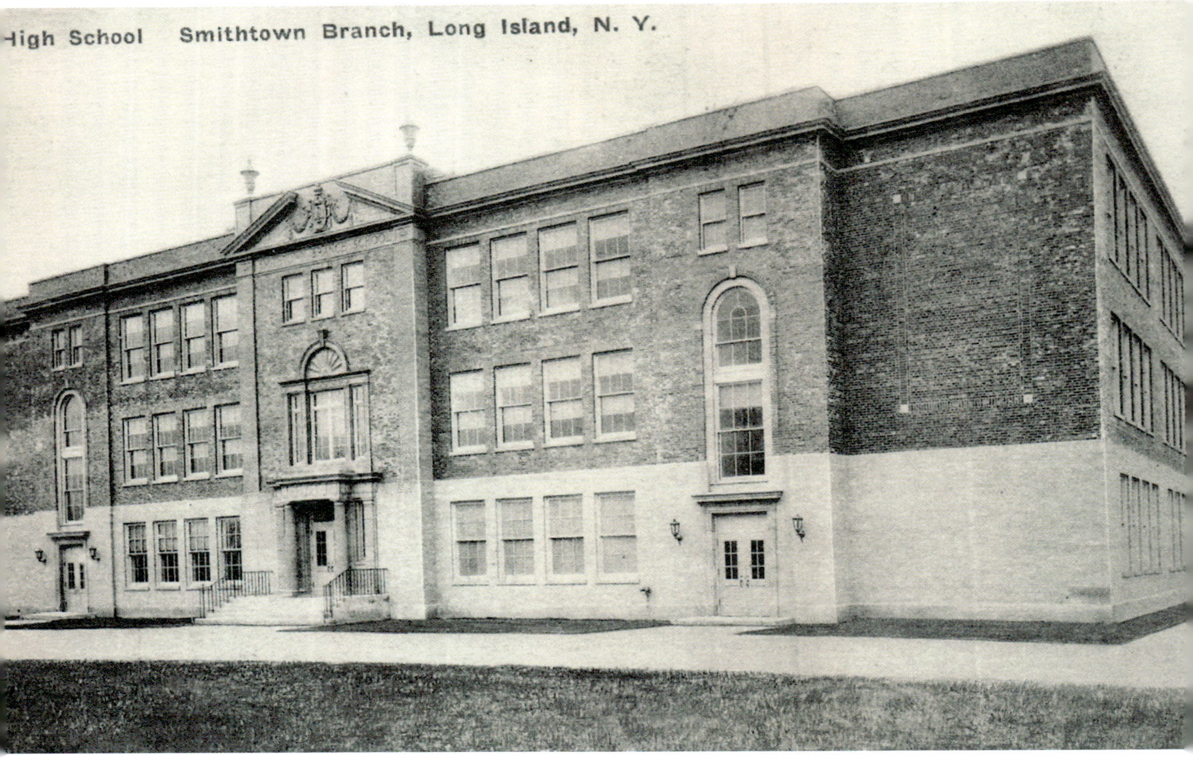

The New York Avenue School opened for classes in the fall of 1925. The school housed grades one through 12 until the 1950s, when enrollment exploded, bringing change. In 1950, the building became a junior/senior high school, and in 1955, it became the Smithtown Central High School. After a new high school in St. James opened in 1959, the New York Avenue School was closed. The building now serves as administrative offices for the Smithtown Central School District.

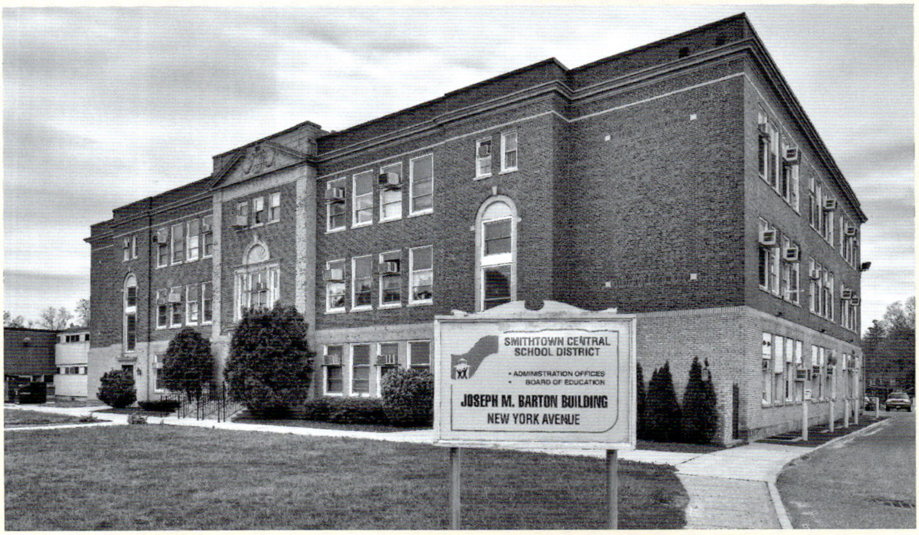

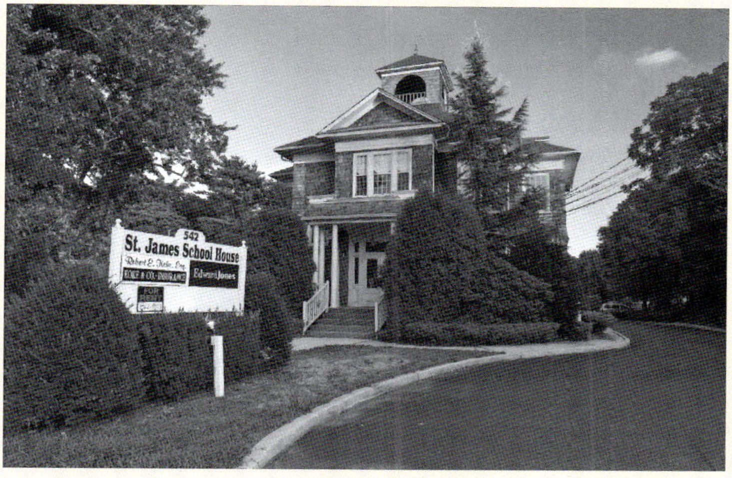

The St. James Public School was built in 1905 to accommodate a population that had outgrown its existing schoolhouse. The two-story, shingle-sided edifice served as St. James's elementary school until the current St. James Elementary School opened in 1939. After it ceased operating as a schoolhouse, the building was renovated (losing its bell tower in the process) and converted into apartment housing. In the 1990s, the structure was restored to its original look and reopened as an office building.

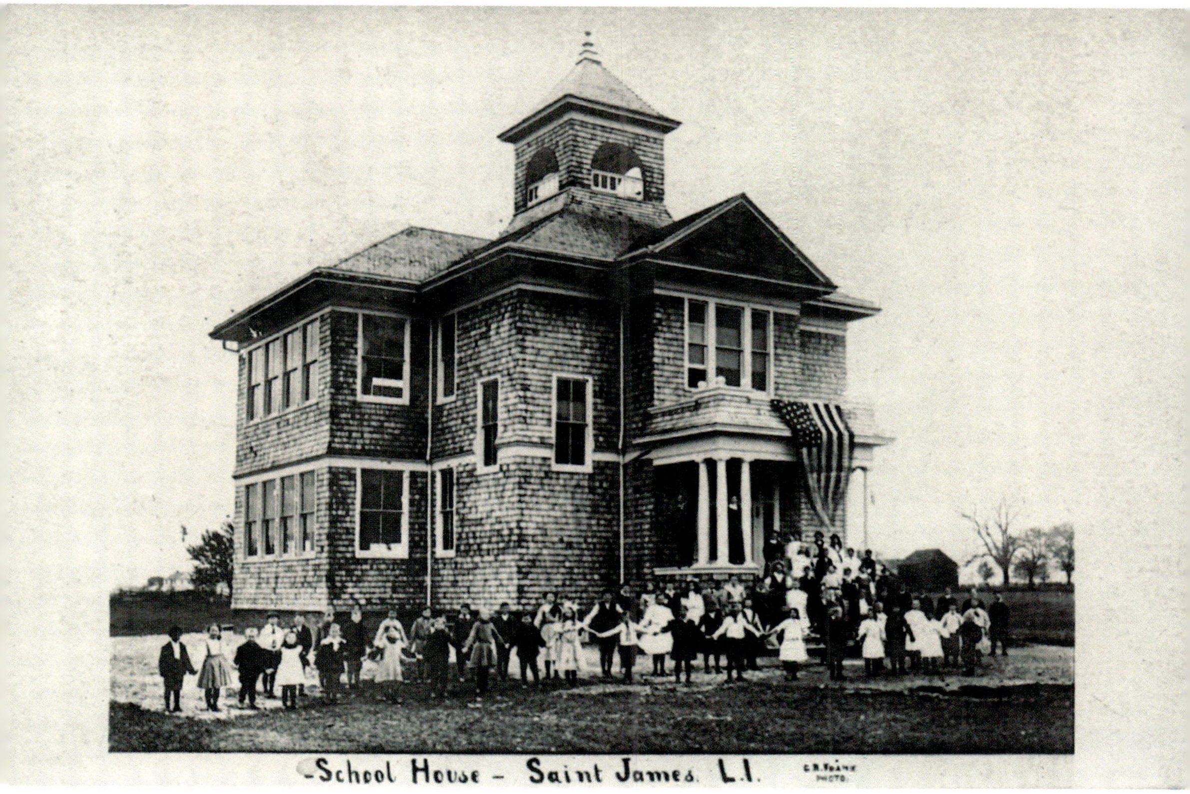

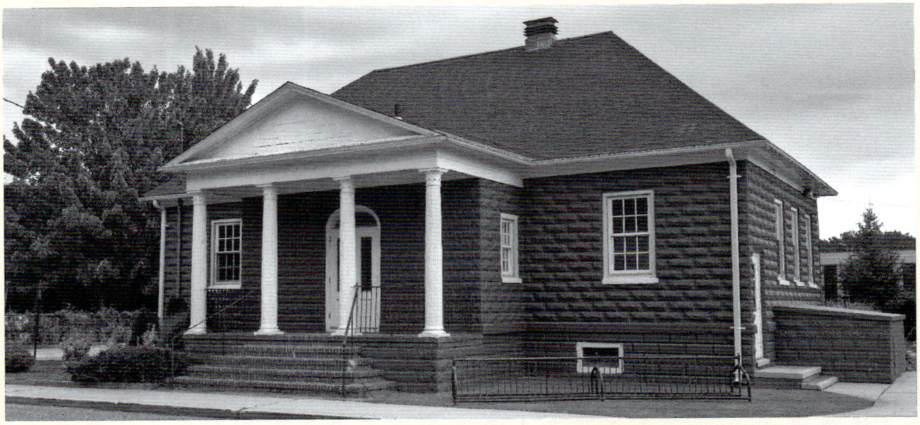

The Nesconset Schoolhouse, a two-room concrete structure located on Gibbs Pond Road near Lake Avenue, first opened its doors in 1906. In her memoirs, longtime Nesconset resident Juliette Kieselstein recalls the primitive conditions of the schoolhouse: "There were no conveniences—running water was supplied by an outside pump and outside privies served as toilets. These were pretty cold in the winter." In 1950, this original schoolhouse was incorporated into the site of the brand-new Nesconset Elementary School. (Historic photograph courtesy Patricia McManus Ward.)

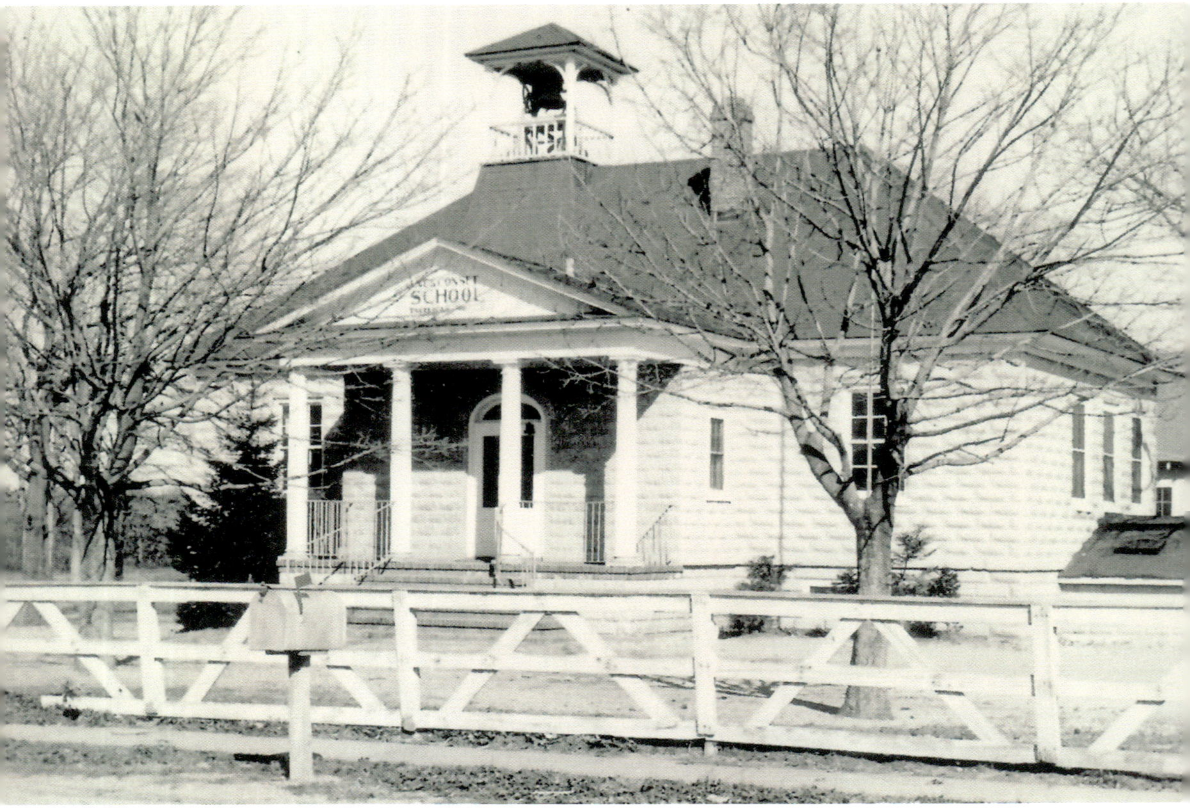

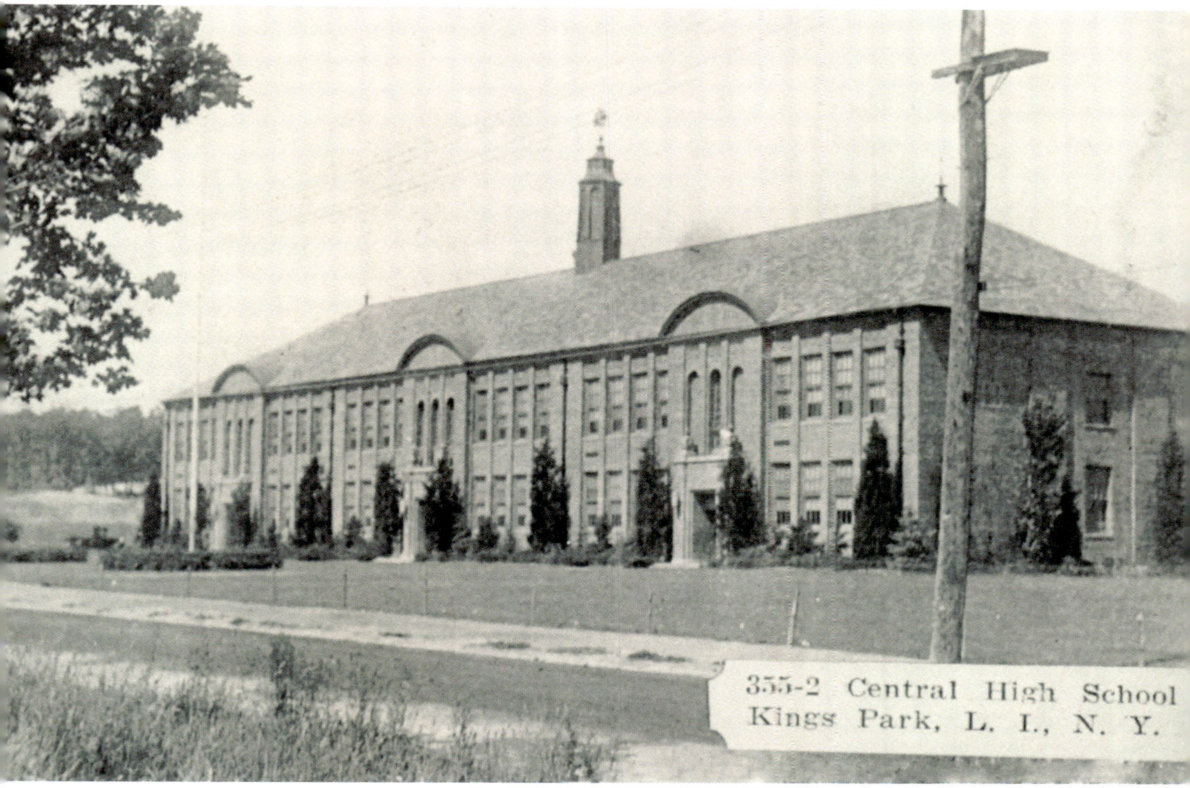

Built in 1928, the Ralph J. Osgood Building on Church Street and Old Dock Road has, at various points in its life, been the community's high school, a middle school, and an elementary school. The building's attractive Art Deco exterior details catch the eye of many an architectural aficionado. Today, the structure houses the Kings Park Heritage Museum.

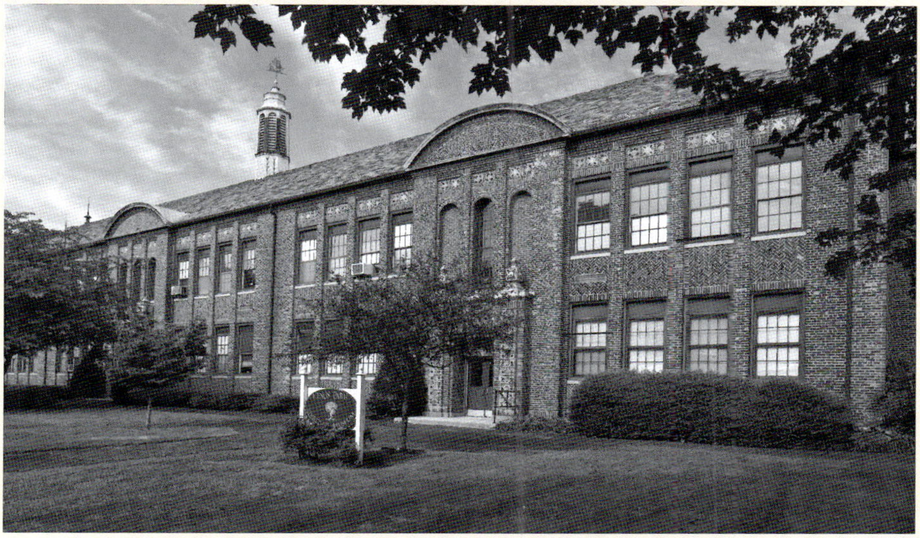

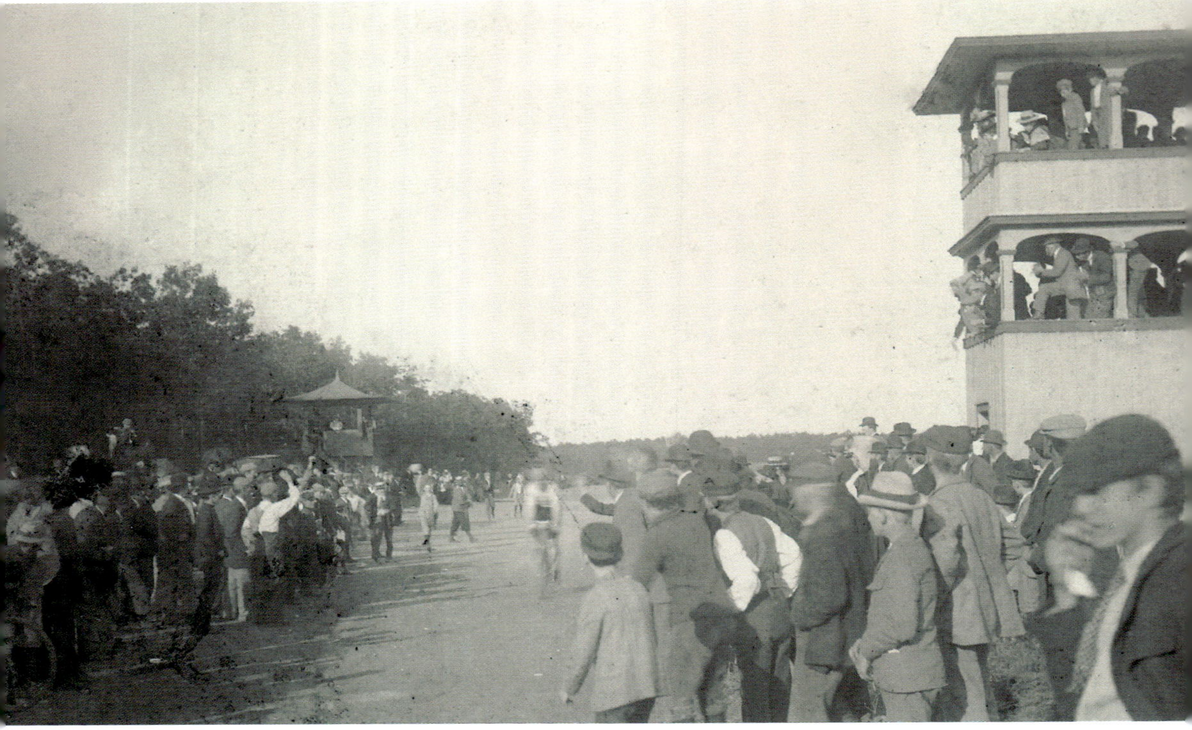

Constructed on the grounds of Carll S. Burr's Indian Head Stock Farm in the 1880s, the Burr Racetrack was the first one-mile trotting track in Suffolk County. While the track initially served as the ideal proving ground for the horses trained at Burr's internationally renowned horse training institute, in later years, the oval hosted a variety of competitions, including bicycle (seen here), motorcycle, and automobile races. The site is now home to Commack High School and its associated track and field venue.

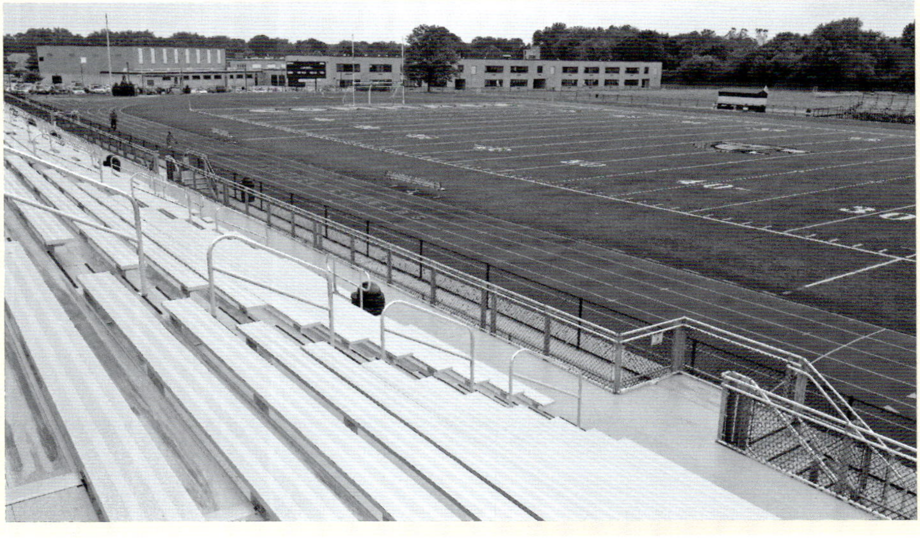

CHAPTER

Turn Left at the Bull

Landmarks Saved and Lost

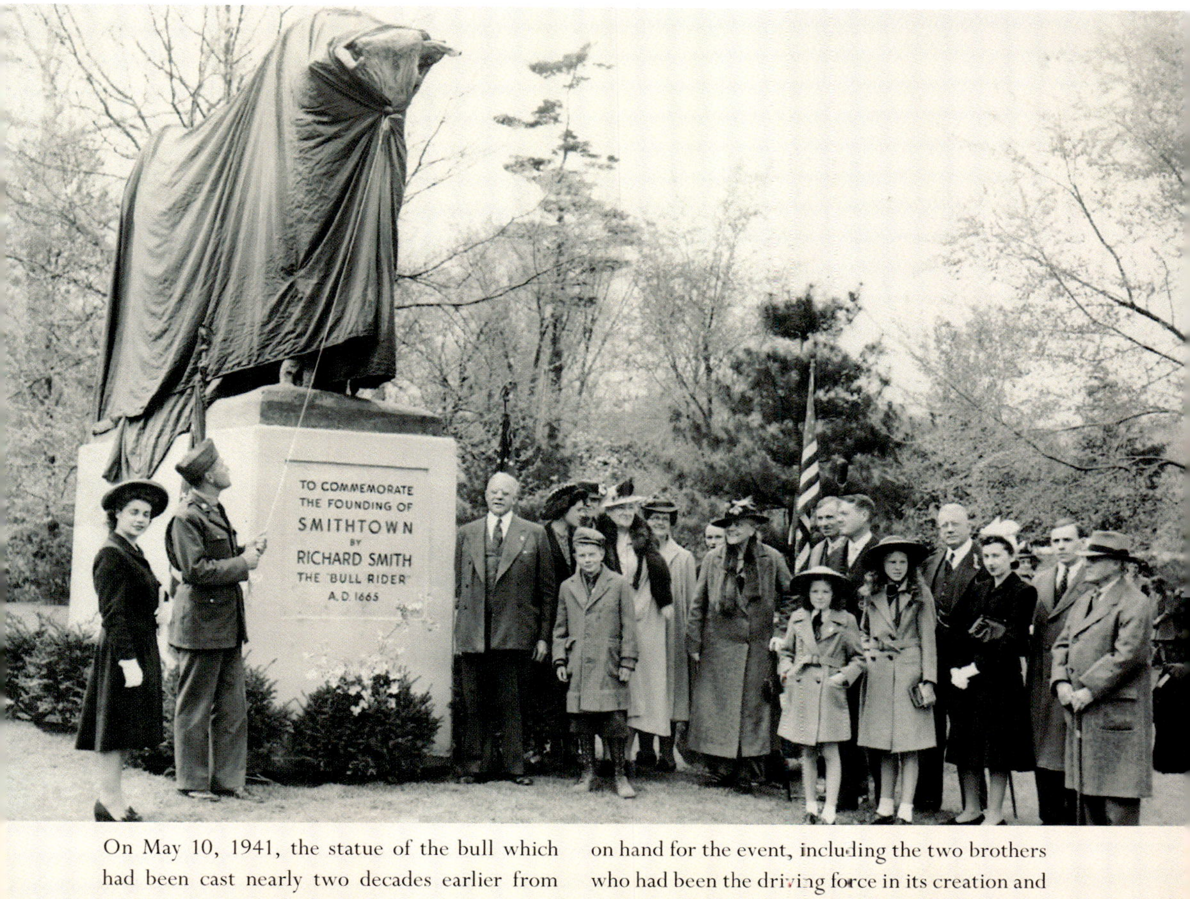

On May 10, 1941, the statue of the bull which had been cast nearly two decades earlier from a sculpted design by Charles Cary Rumsey was unveiled to Smithtown's residents in Head of the River Park. Many Smith family descendants were on hand for the event, including the two brothers who had been the driving force in its creation and erection, Lawrence Smith Butler and Charles Stewart Butler.

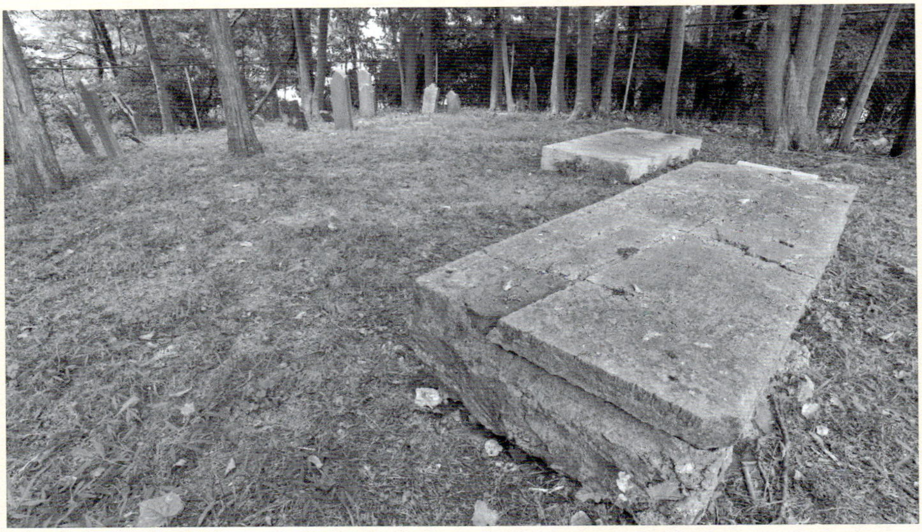

The Patentee's Graveyard in Nissequogue is located on Whisper Hill, which lies to the north of the intersection of River and Moriches Roads. Many believe that Richard Smythe, the patentee of Smithtown, is buried on the hill next to his son Obadiah, whose gravesite is seen in the 1895 photograph included here. Since Richard's grave was never marked, Smith family descendants commemorated his life by placing a granite table-stone near Obadiah's grave in 1900.

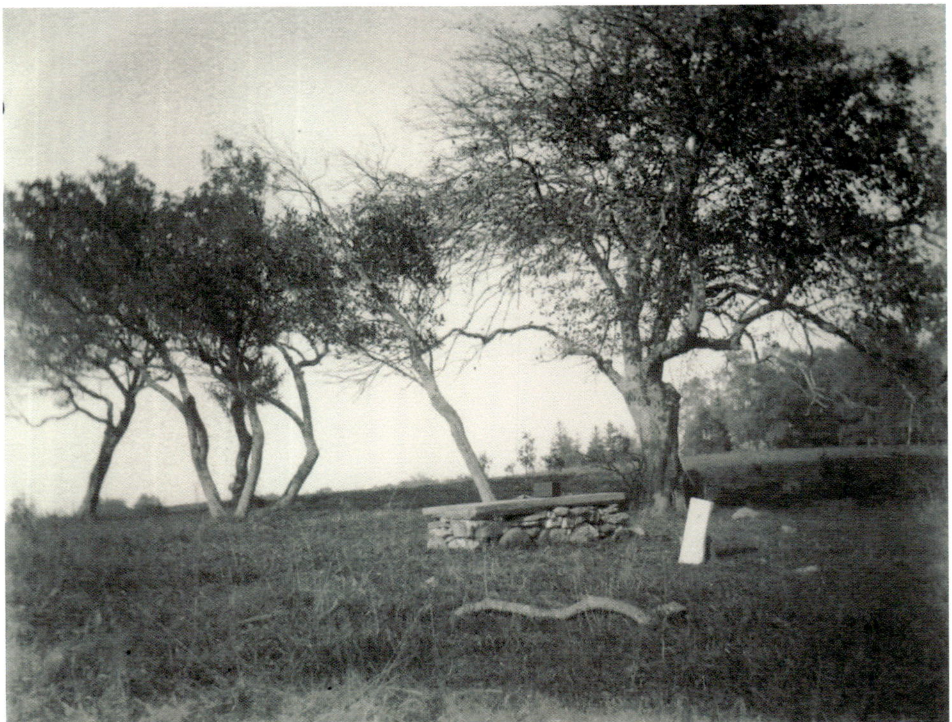

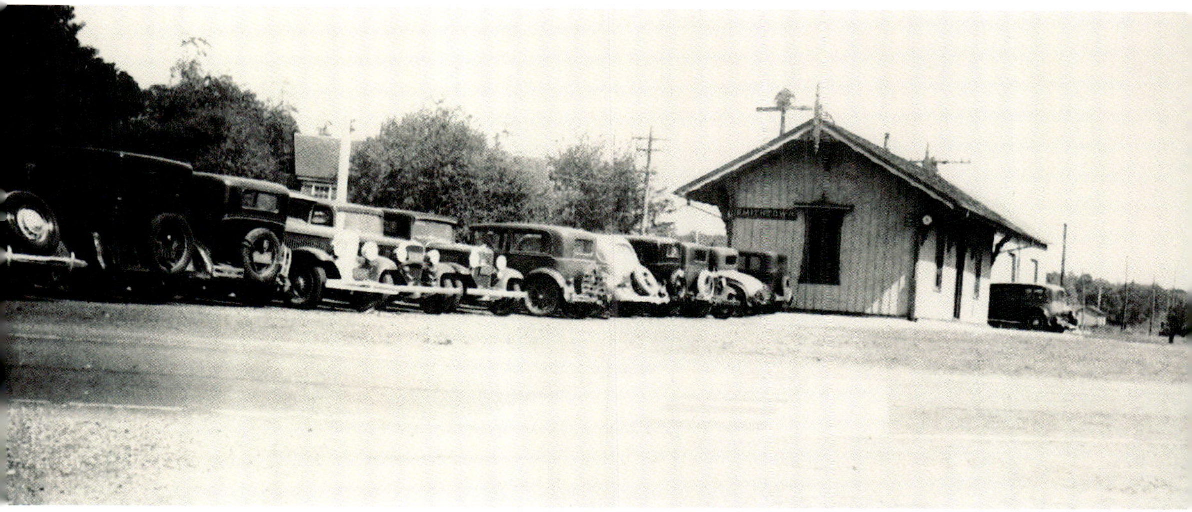

The original Smithtown Railroad Station was built in 1872, when the LIRR was extended to Smithtown. A new railroad station was built in 1936 while a Works Progress Administration (WPA) project was underway to eliminate the grade-level railroad crossing on Smithtown's Main Street. Lawrence Grant White designed the new station, contractors built it in record time, and it was dedicated on February 20, 1937. The old station was sold to Theodore Bunce, who moved it to Lawrence Avenue.

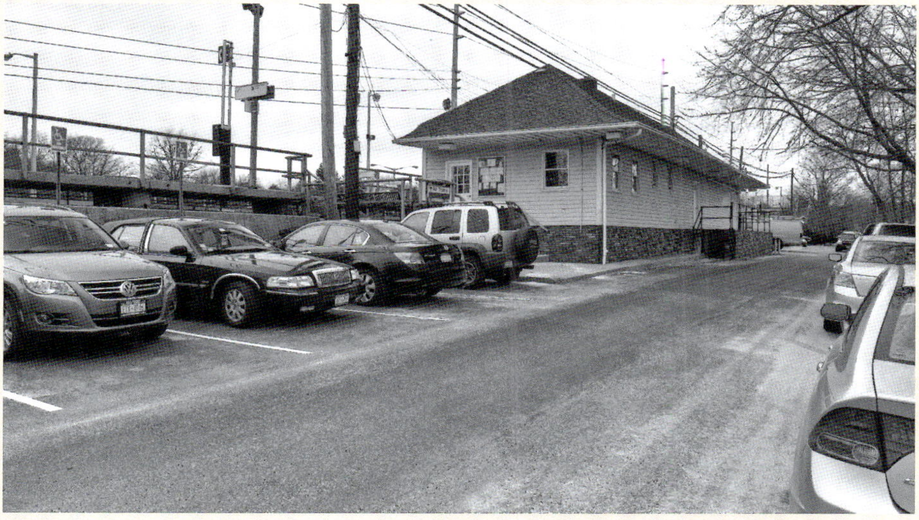

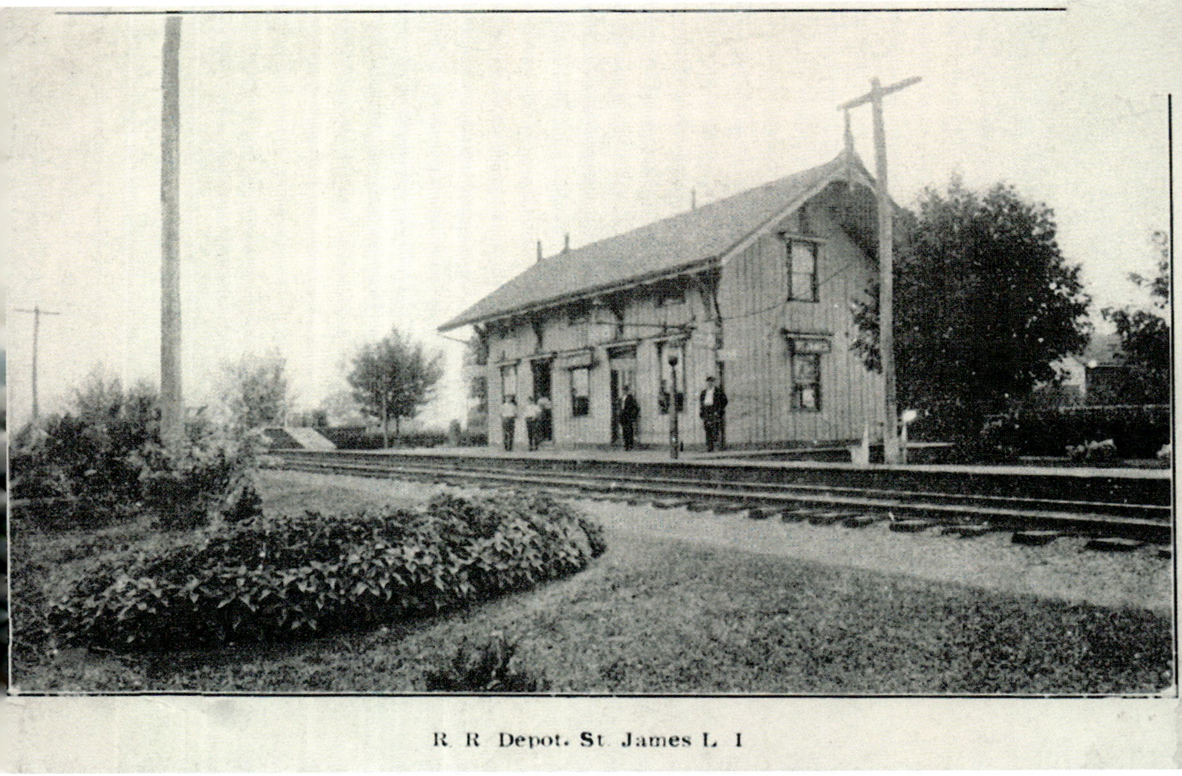

Sitting on the northwest corner of the Lake and Railroad Avenues intersection, the St. James Railroad Station is one of the oldest existing station houses associated with the Long Island Railroad. Paid for and built by local residents, the station opened in 1873 as the LIRR expanded service beyond its former eastern terminus at Northport. Though it had fallen into a state of disrepair by the 1980s, the landmark, amid much community support, was successfully restored during the early 1990s.

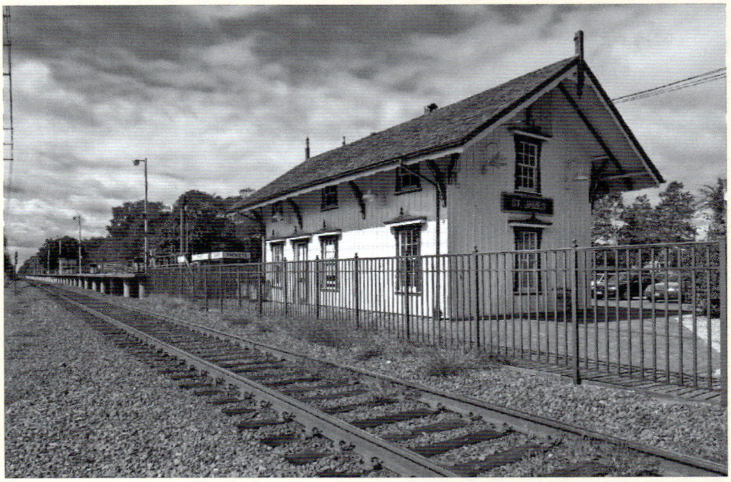

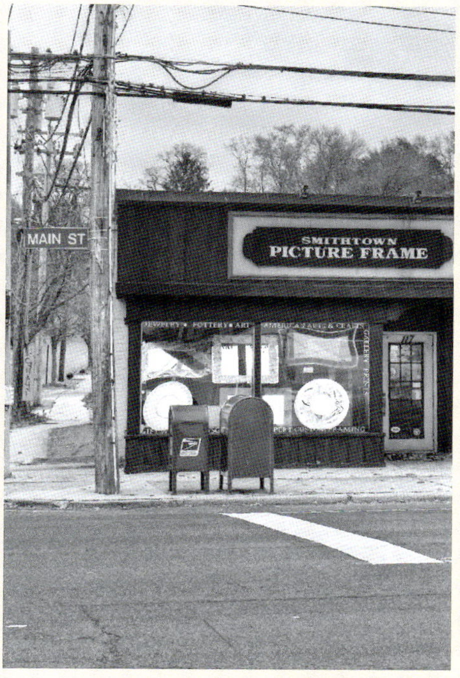

The Smithtown Branch Post Office, located on the northeast corner of Main Street and Bellemeade Avenue, is seen here in the 1930s. There were actually two post offices in Smithtown when this photograph was taken: one at Head of the River and this one in Smithtown Branch. In 1952, the federal government merged the two post offices and located the single Smithtown Post Office in this building. The current Smithtown Post Office, located on Route 111, was built in 1967. (Historic photograph courtesy Lee Corbani.)

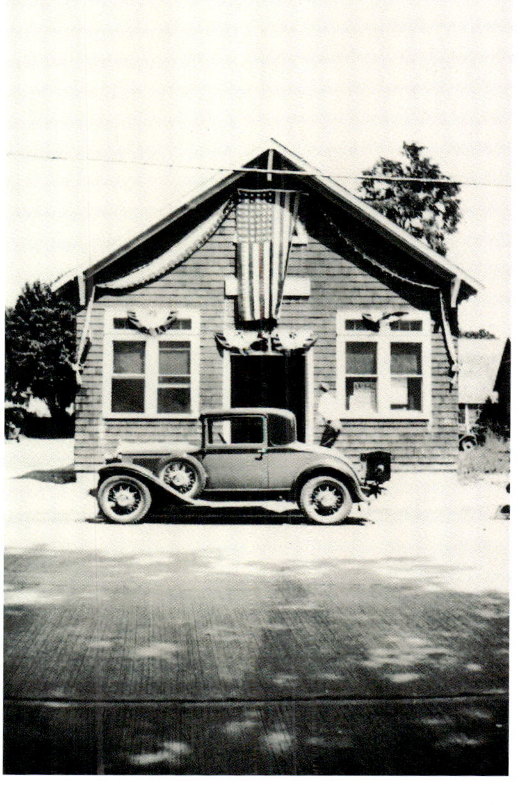

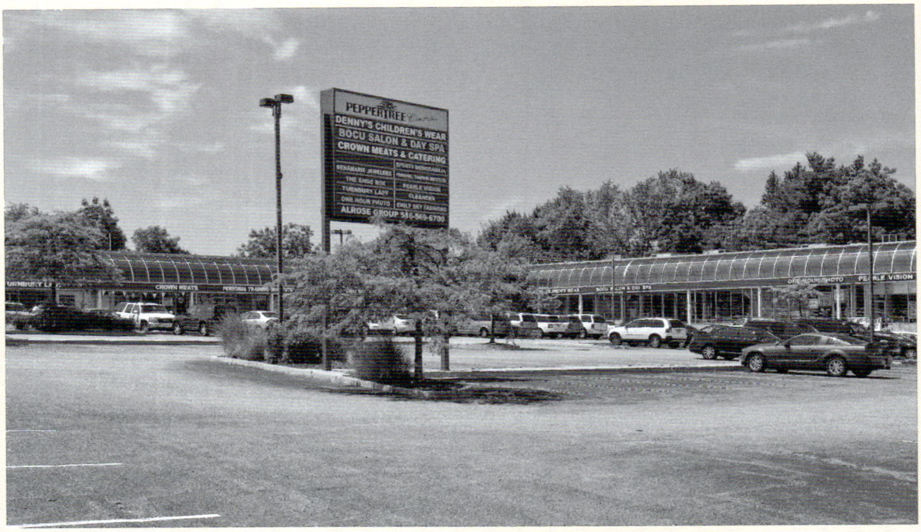

The Commack General Store stood on the northwest corner of Commack/Townline Road and Jericho Turnpike, where Peppertree Commons is located today. This photograph was taken around 1905, when Frank Otten owned and operated the store and post office. Not long after this photograph was taken, the general store installed gas pumps in front of the building. The store served the residents of Commack until the early 1960s, when the crossroads intersection was redesigned and the building was demolished.

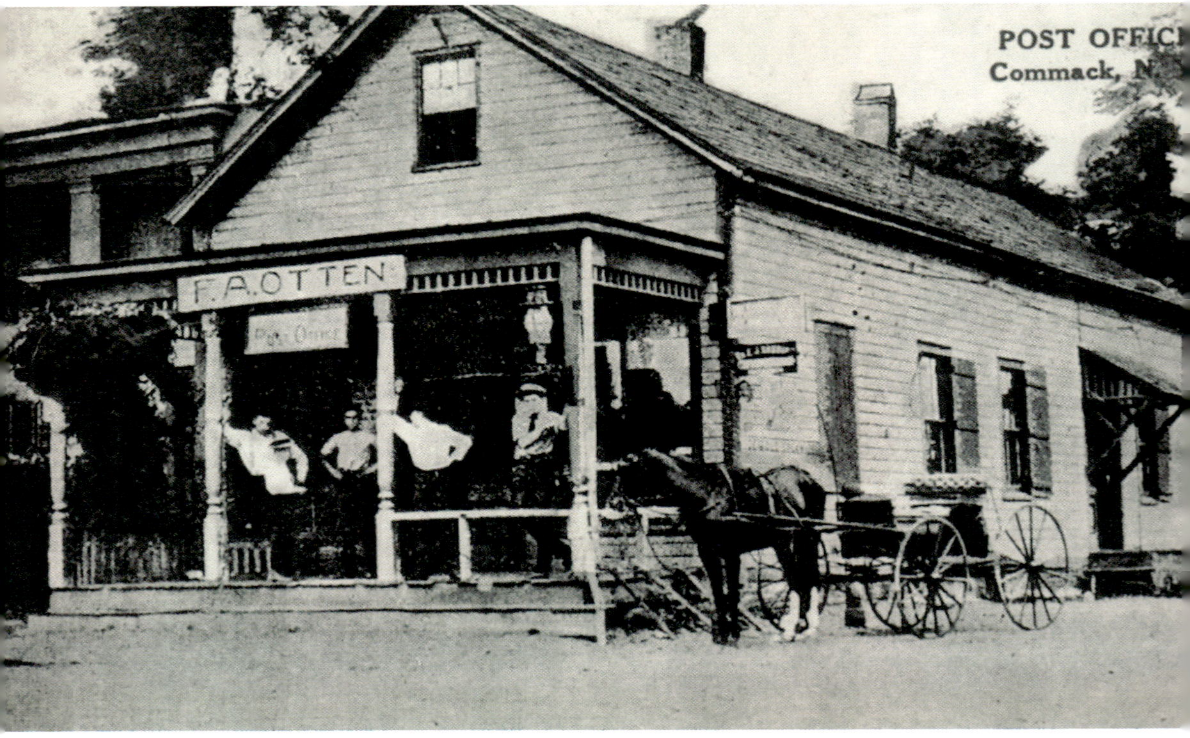

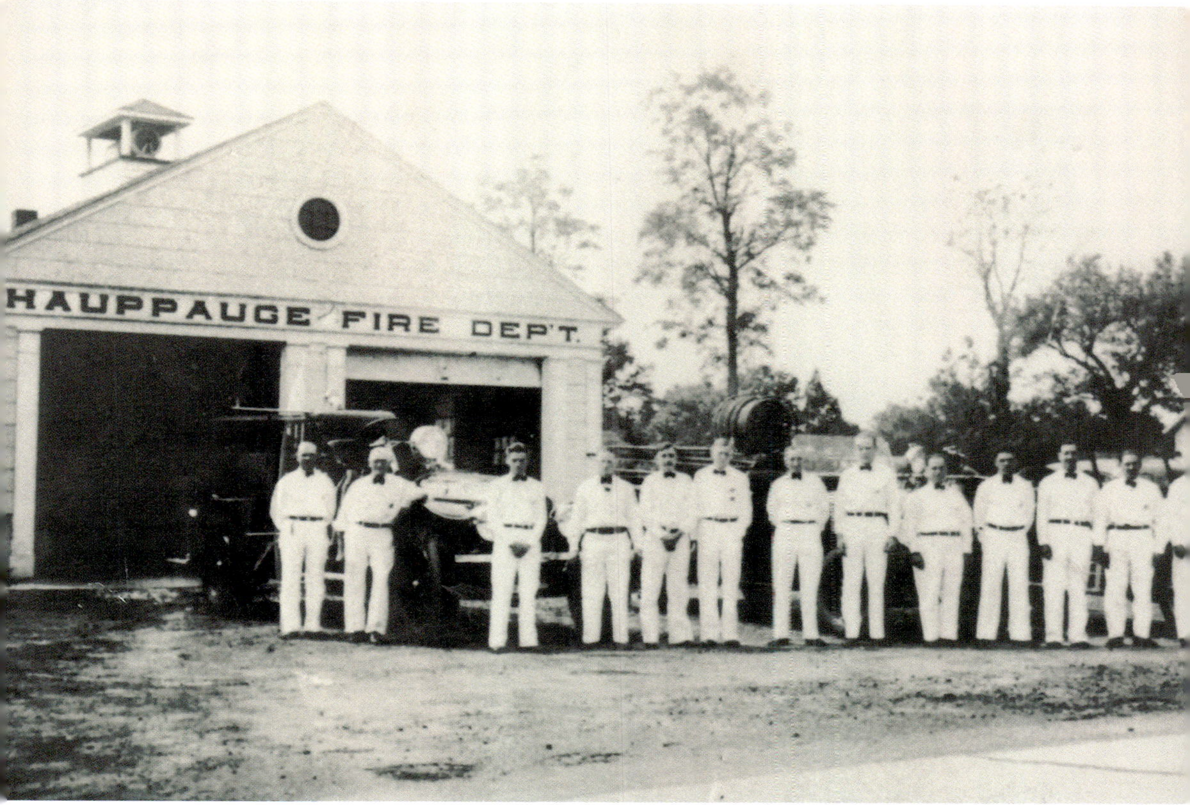

Concern over forest fires aroused community efforts to begin a volunteer fire company in Hauppauge in 1931. Several years prior to this, a small fire protection association used Ford Model As to patrol the vicinity, on the lookout for conflagrations in the heavily wooded area. The first Hauppauge District Fire House on Route 111 received several major additions in the mid-1950s and in 1970. (Historic photograph courtesy Greg Gottlieb, Hauppauge Fire Department.)

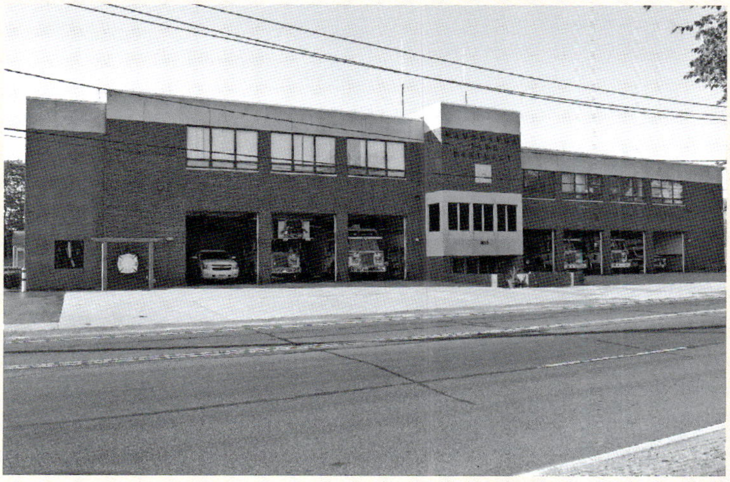

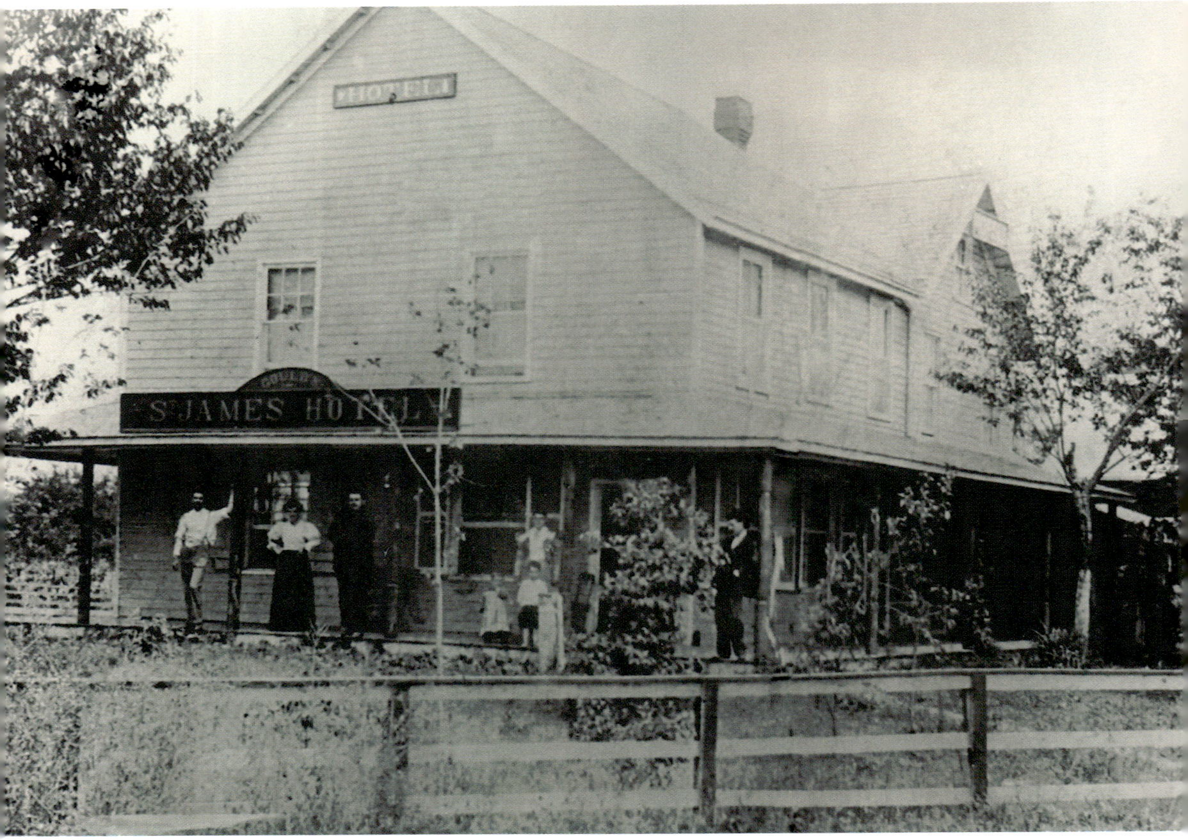

Built to accommodate the flood of tourists who came to the area following the LIRR's extension in 1872, the St. James Hotel once stood on the triangle of ground directly opposite the St. James Firehouse (built in 1923). The hotel was at one time a favorite haunt of members of the actors' colony, including "Gentleman Jim" Corbett. More recently, the building became the Gold Coast Two and was doing a lively bar trade until it burned down in the 1970s.

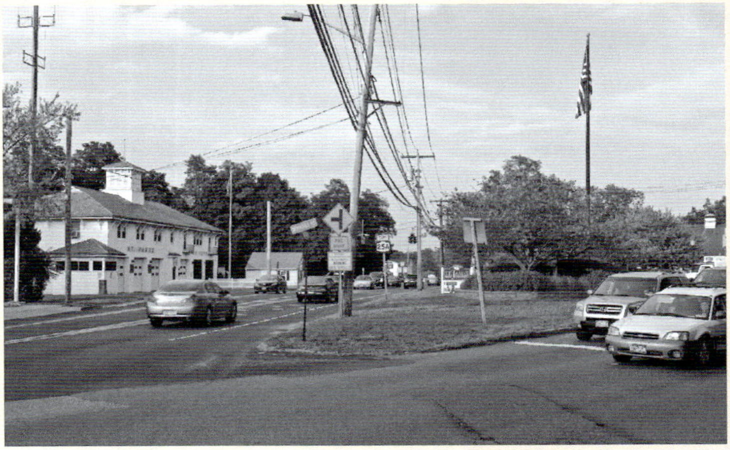

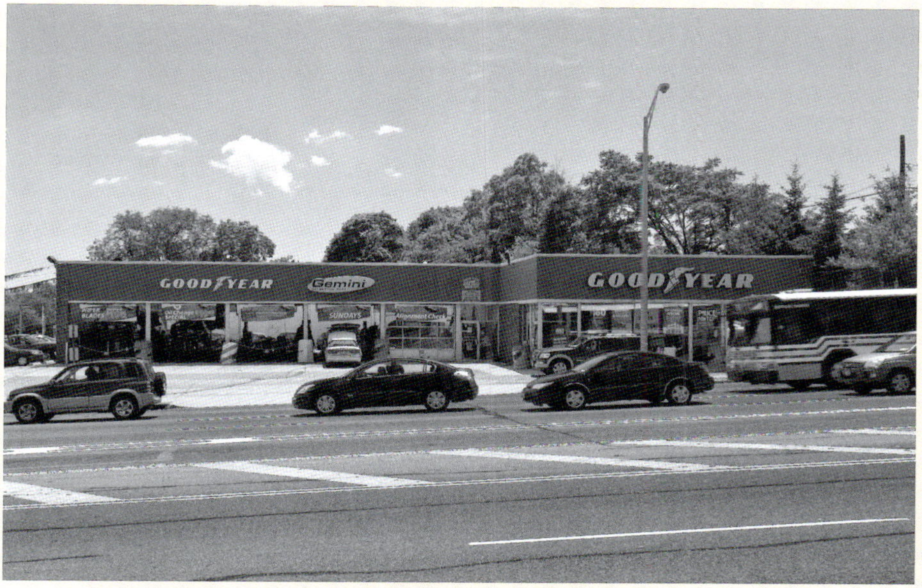

Built in the 1880s, the Commack Hotel stood on the southwest corner of the intersection of Jericho Turnpike and Commack/Townline Road. At the turn of the 20th century, the hotel catered to visitors who came to the little crossroads village to watch trotting races at Carll S. Burr's racetrack. The hotel remained a landmark in Commack Corners until it burned to the ground in 1965. Today, a Goodyear tire center occupies the corner.

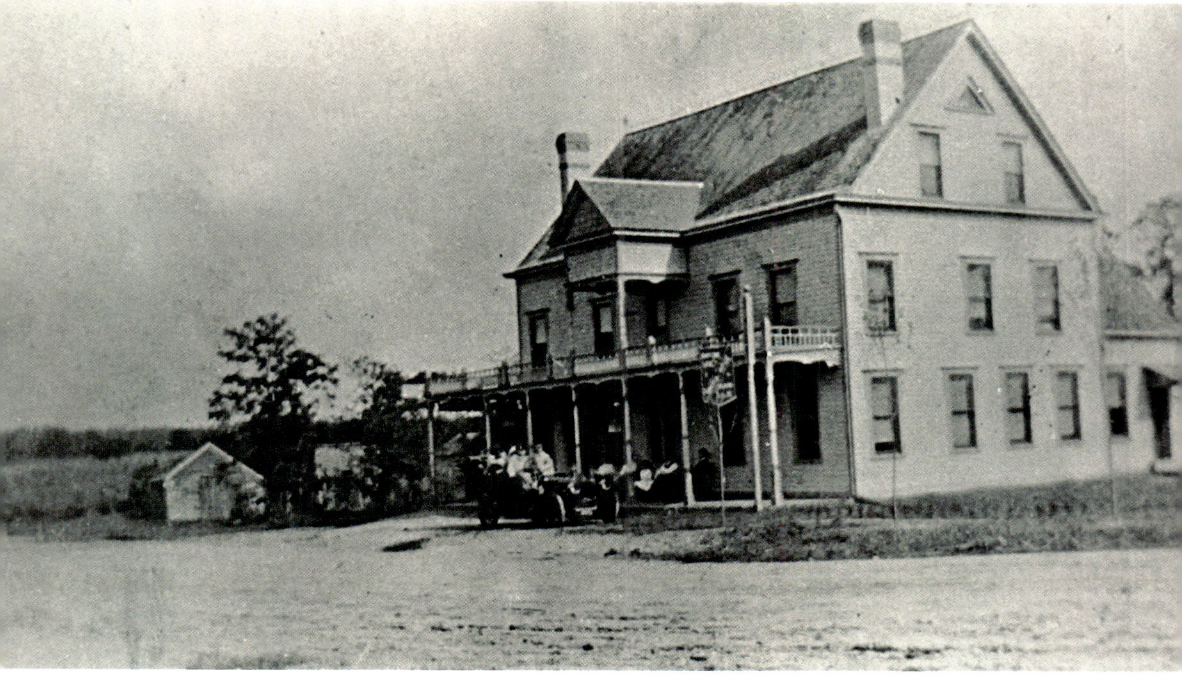

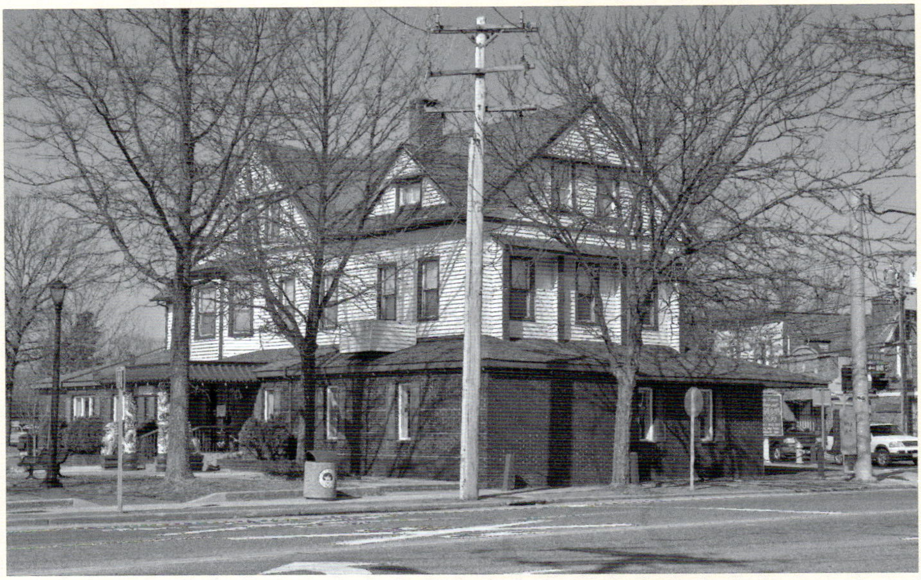

Kings Park was recognized as "Brooklyn East" after the major psychiatric hospital for Brooklyn patients became the center of the community. This building, at the corner of Main Street and Indian Head Road, maintains many of its features from 1894. It was originally the 22-guest-capacity Brooklyn Hotel, an establishment run by a retired New York City Fire Department captain, George Henry Cusick. Cusick's family owned the structure until 1946. Since then, various eateries have called this building home.

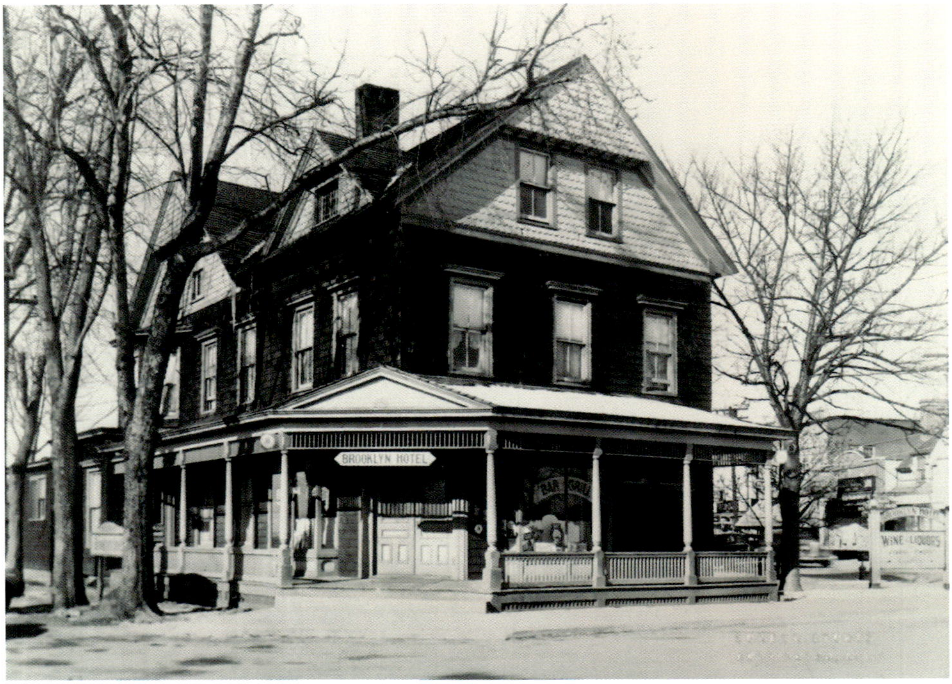

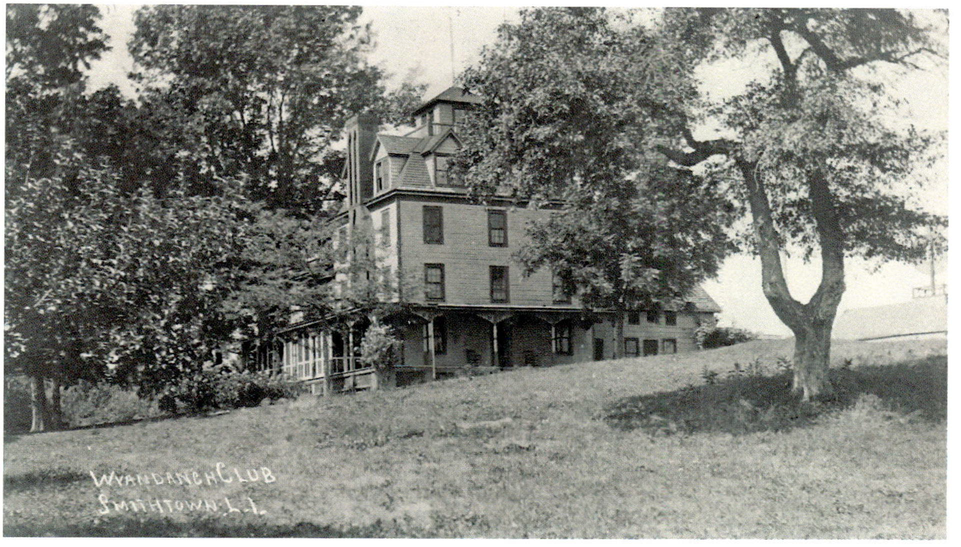

Built originally as the home of Caleb Smith I (1724–1800), the center section of this building dates to the early 1750s. After purchasing the house in 1888, the Wyandanch Club enlarged the structure to its present configuration in order to render it a more suitable clubhouse for their 600-acre hunting and fishing retreat. Owned by New York State since 1963, the building currently houses the Caleb Smith State Park Preserve Nature Museum. (Historic photograph courtesy Smithtown Library, Diane Simonson Collection.)

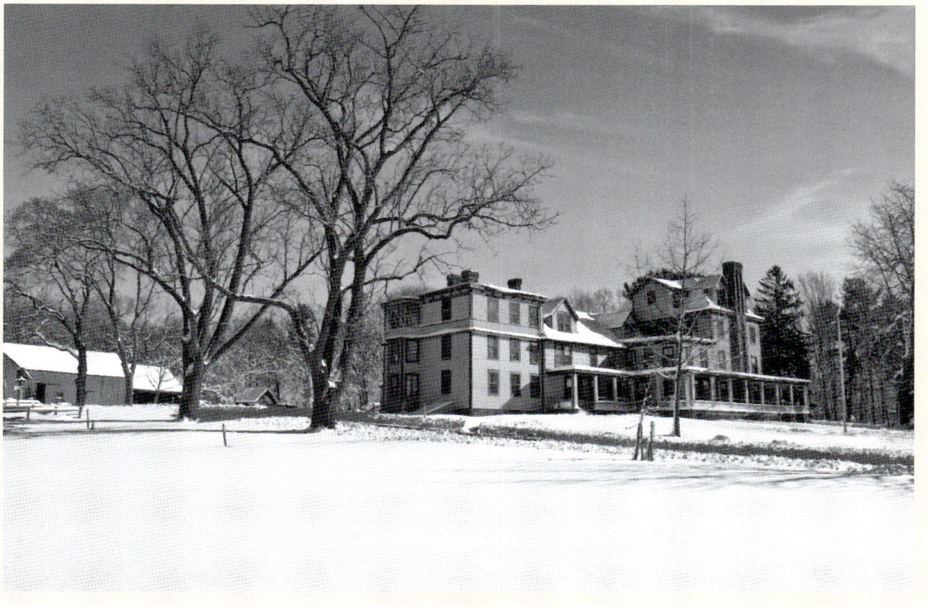

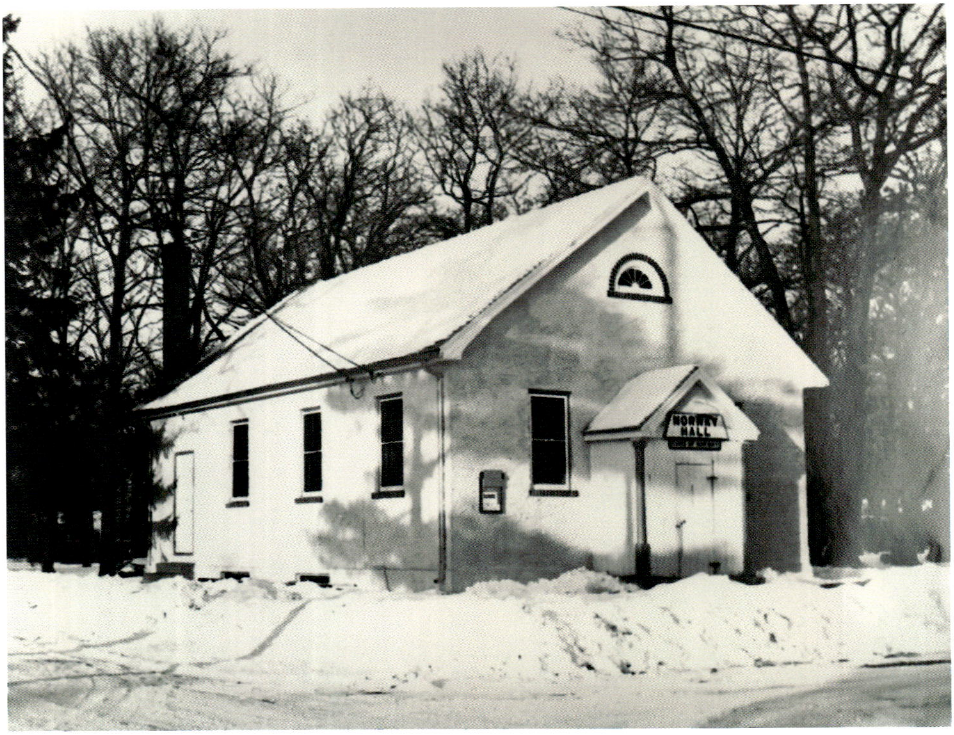

A significant influx of Norwegians relocated to Smithtown from Brooklyn, Manhattan, and Staten Island in the early 1900s. In 1924, this burgeoning population formed Sons of Norway Loyal Lodge No. 252 and began holding regular meetings and social activities in Mechanics Hall (now VFW Hall) in St. James. By 1930, the group had gathered enough resources to build Norway Hall on the corner of Seventh Street and Fourth Avenue in the grid-like area once known as St. James Park.

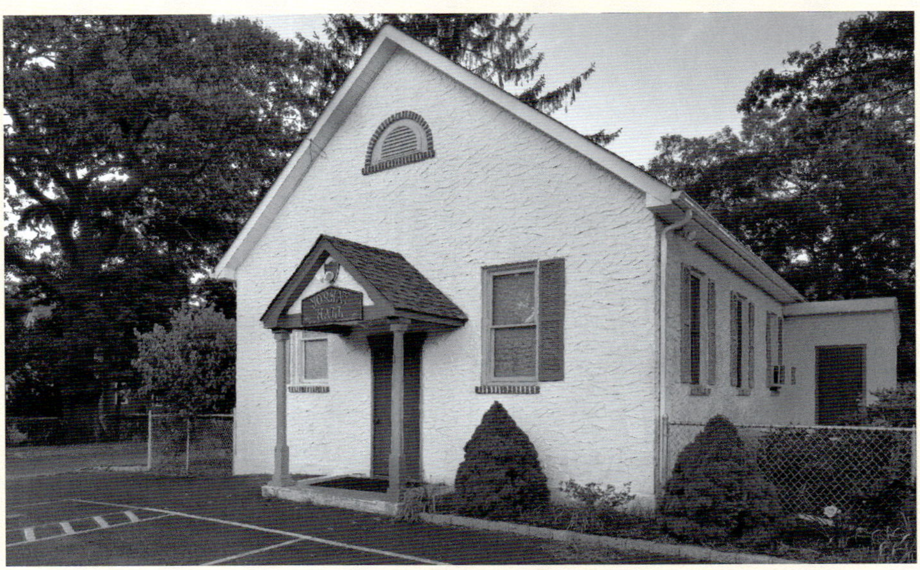

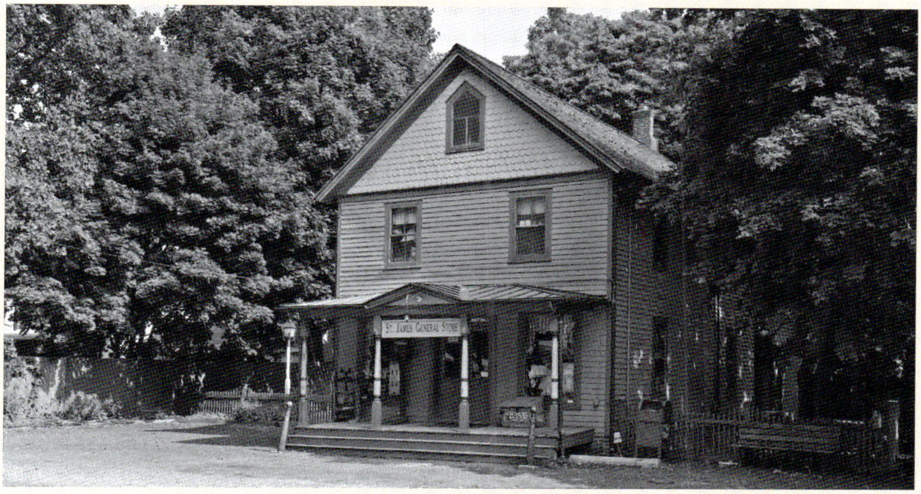

Built in 1857 and listed on the National Register of Historic Places, the St. James General Store had only five owners in its lifetime before being bought by Suffolk County in 1990. Shortly thereafter, the store was returned to the original colors Ebenezer Smith had painted it—bright yellow, pumpkin orange, and olive green—during a restoration project. The Smithtown Historical Society owns many of the store's account books from the late 1800s and early 1900s.

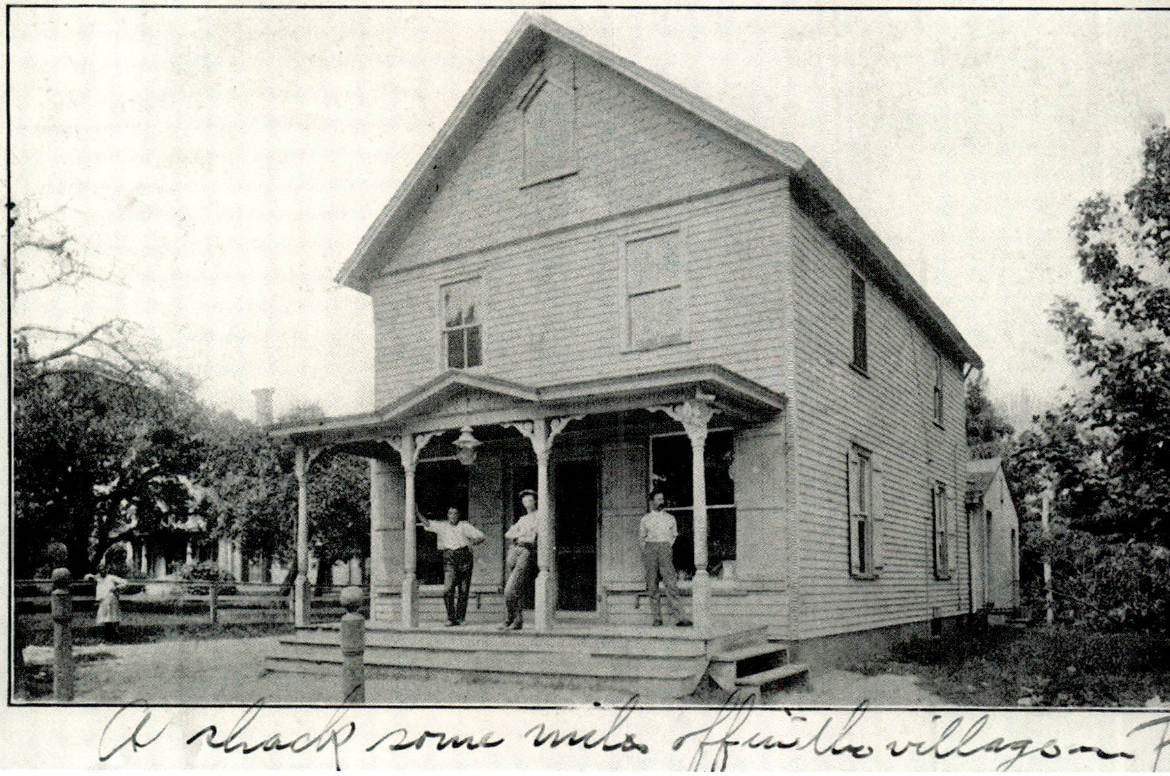

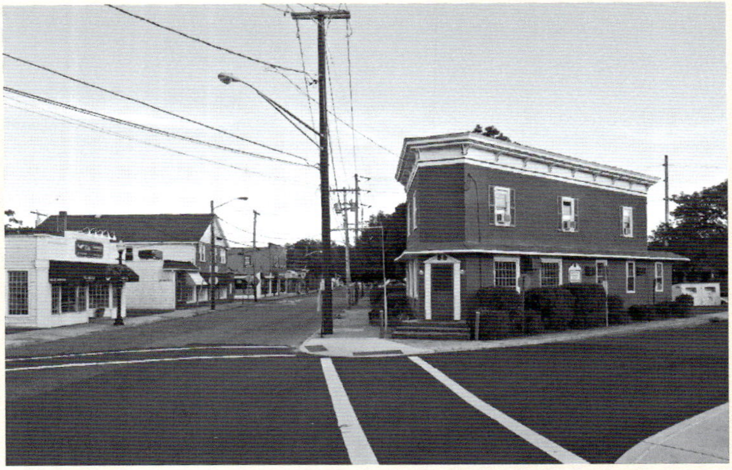

A 1980s historic restoration project removed this building's modern siding to reveal some of its more elegant historic details. The structure was built by Joseph Amey in 1908, just a few years after New York City's more famous Flatiron Building (named for its triangular shape). Over the years, it contained a diverse lot of businesses and functions: a soda fountain, a bowling alley, and a bakery. Today, it is home to an insurance agency.

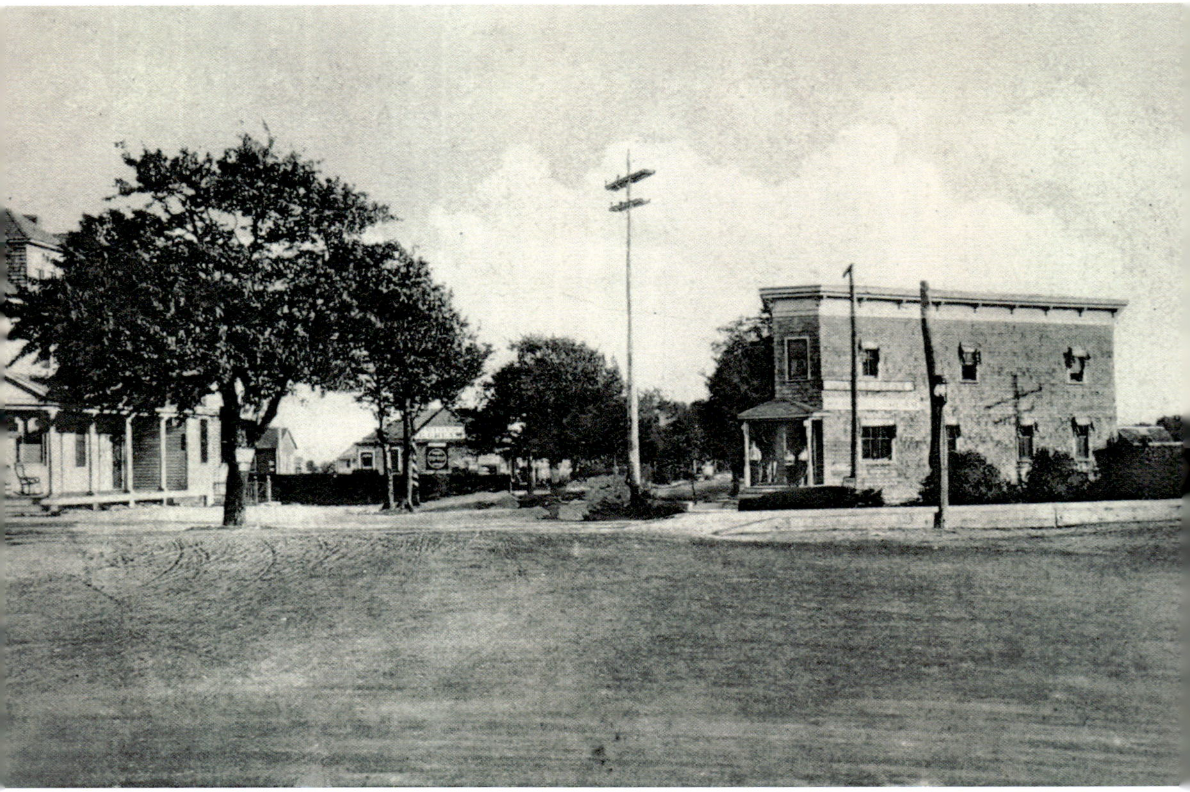

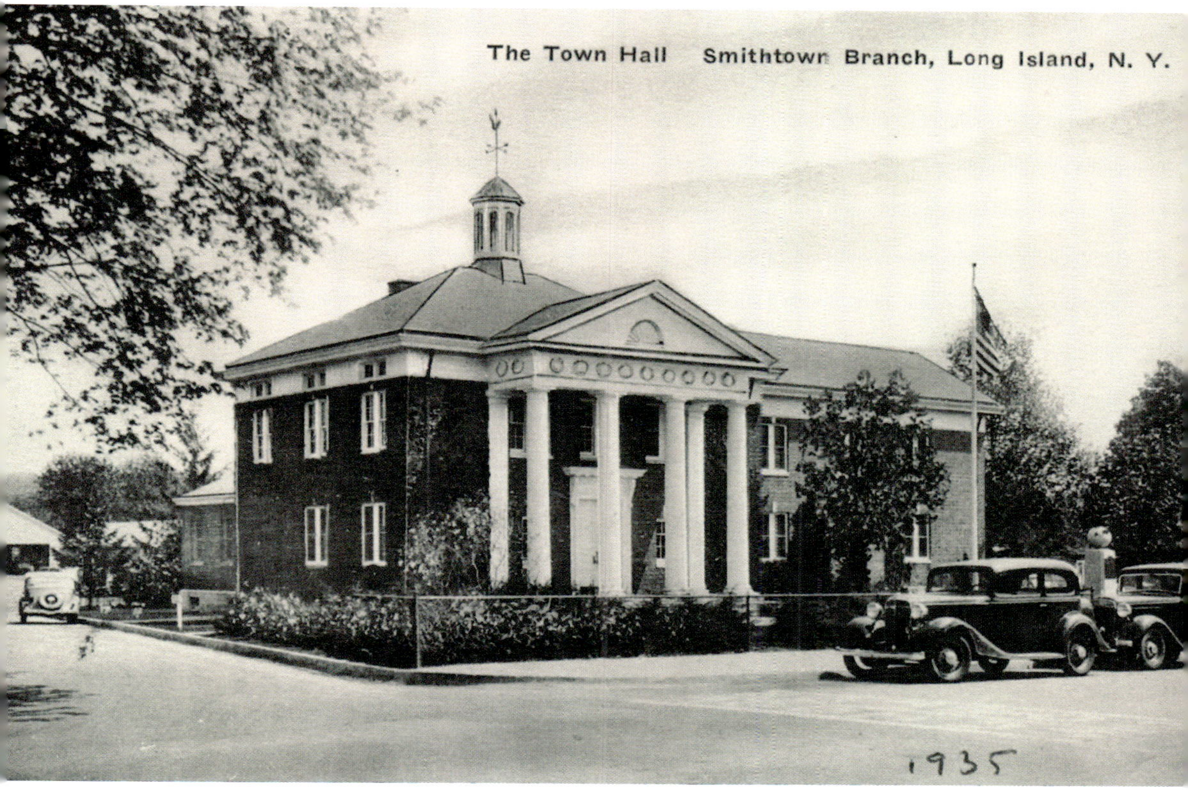

Smithtown Town Hall looks today much like it did in 1935 after the east wing had been added. The 1935 postcard shows the highway department garages tucked behind the building. Those garages now house the Smithtown Planning Department. The little building projecting off the back of town hall was added when the east wing was constructed, and it became the headquarters of the Smithtown Police Department, complete with a squad room, an office for Chief Sy Donnelly, and jail cells.

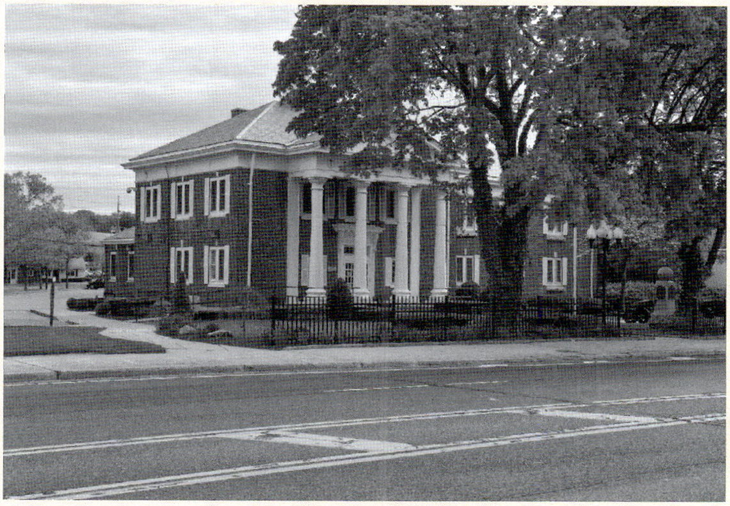

The National Bank of Smithtown Branch first opened in July 1910 in this modest one-room structure. It did not take long for the newborn bank to outgrow its original building. By 1925, the newly named Bank of Smithtown moved several blocks west on Main Street into the much grander edifice it occupies today. While the booming business relocated, the original structure was left standing. After having undergone a series of renovations, it now serves as Dr. Keith Dworkin's optometry office.

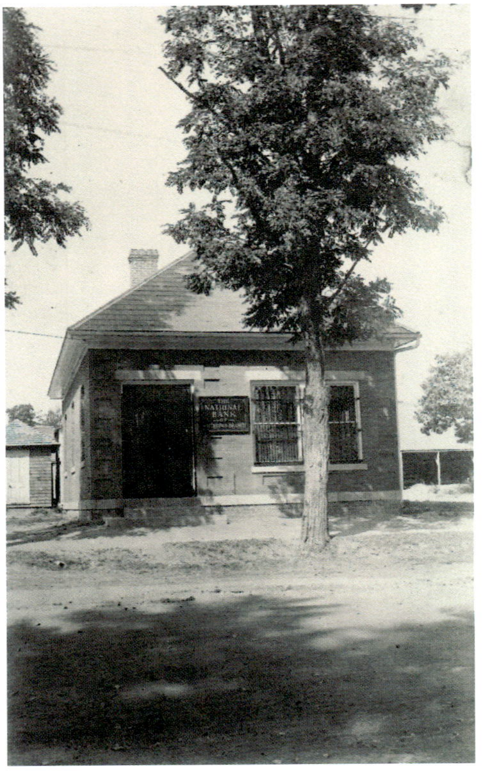

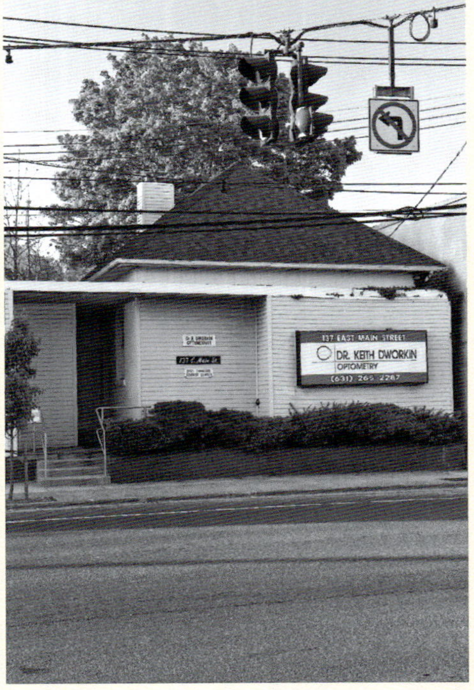

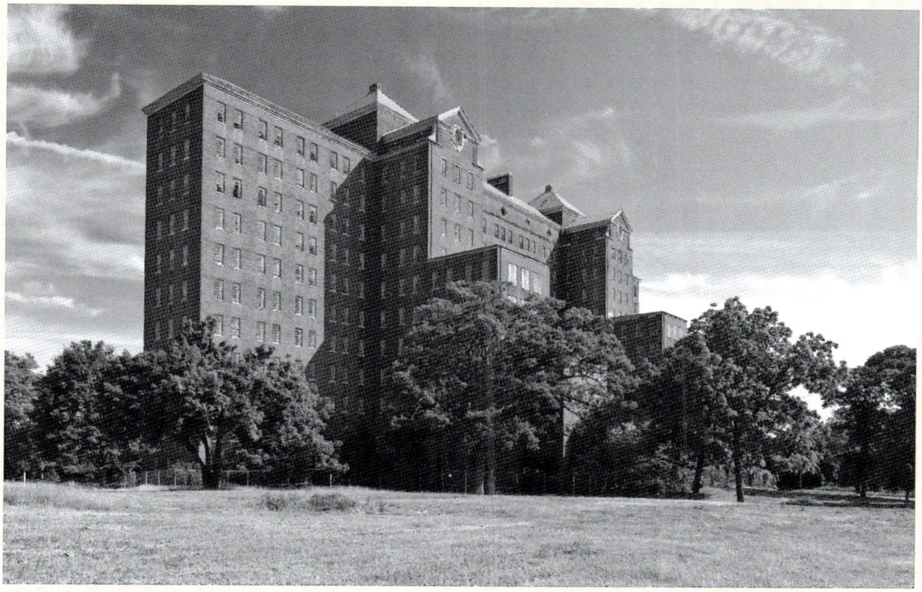

The Kings Park State Hospital Infirmary, Building 93, was constructed as a WPA project in the late 1930s. The 12-story infirmary housed patients according to their mobility: the ambulatory were placed on the ground floors, semi-invalids on the intermediate floors, and the bedridden on the top floors. The white building in the foreground of the 1973 photograph housed the hospital's community store. The smaller building behind the store is a four-lane bowling alley. Today, Building 93 stands vacant awaiting demolition. (Historic photograph courtesy Kings Park Heritage Museum.)

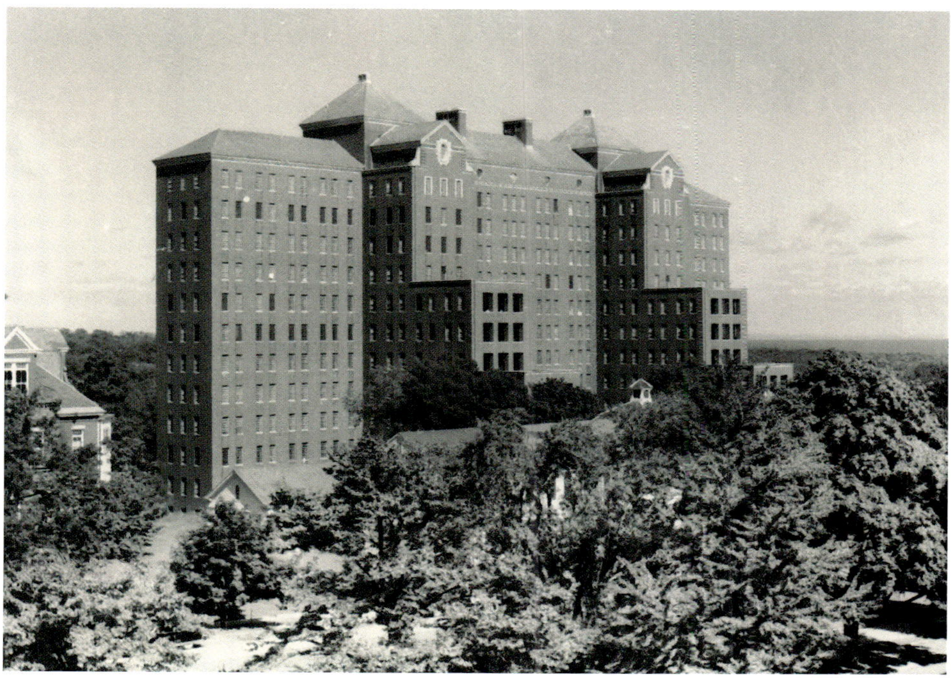

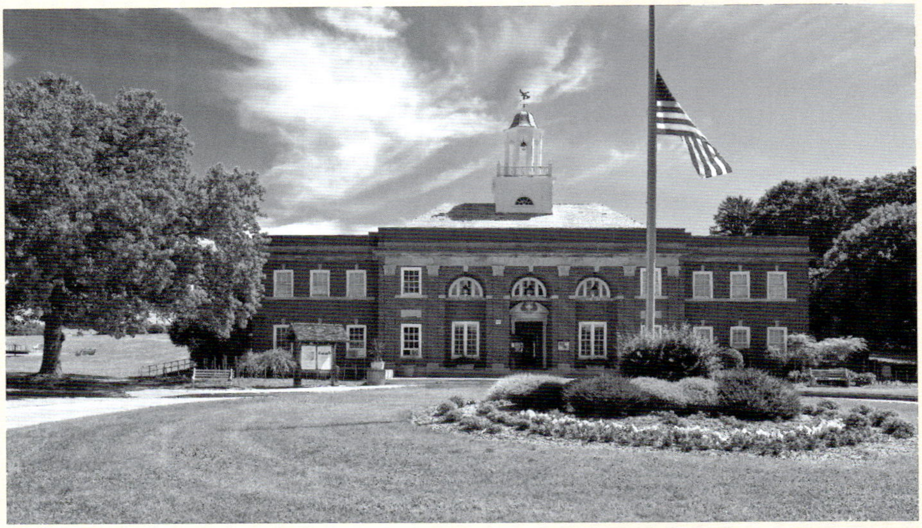

Constructed at the eastern edge of the sprawling Kings Park State Hospital complex in the 1920s, Veterans Memorial Hospital provided care and treatment to mentally disabled veterans until after World War II. After the Kings Park Psychiatric Center (KPPC) closed in 1996, the former hospital, along with many other KPPC buildings, was abandoned. In 1999, the State of New York reopened the building as the headquarters of the newly created Nissequogue River State Park.

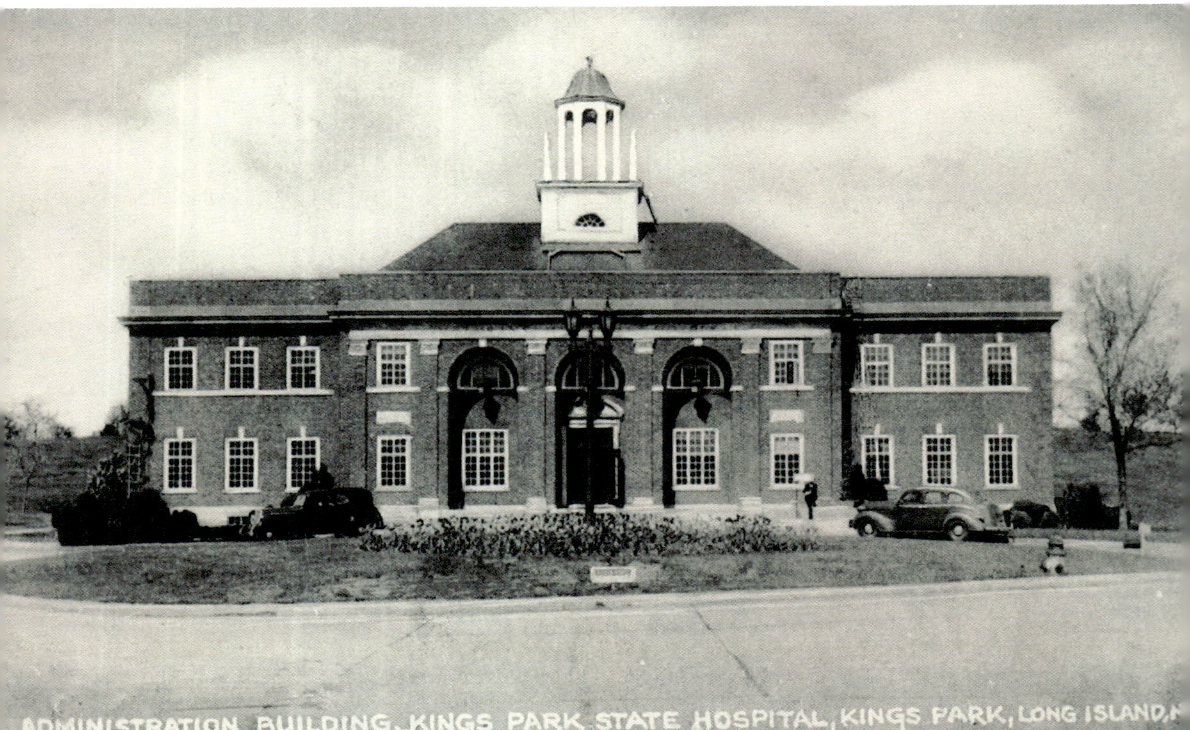

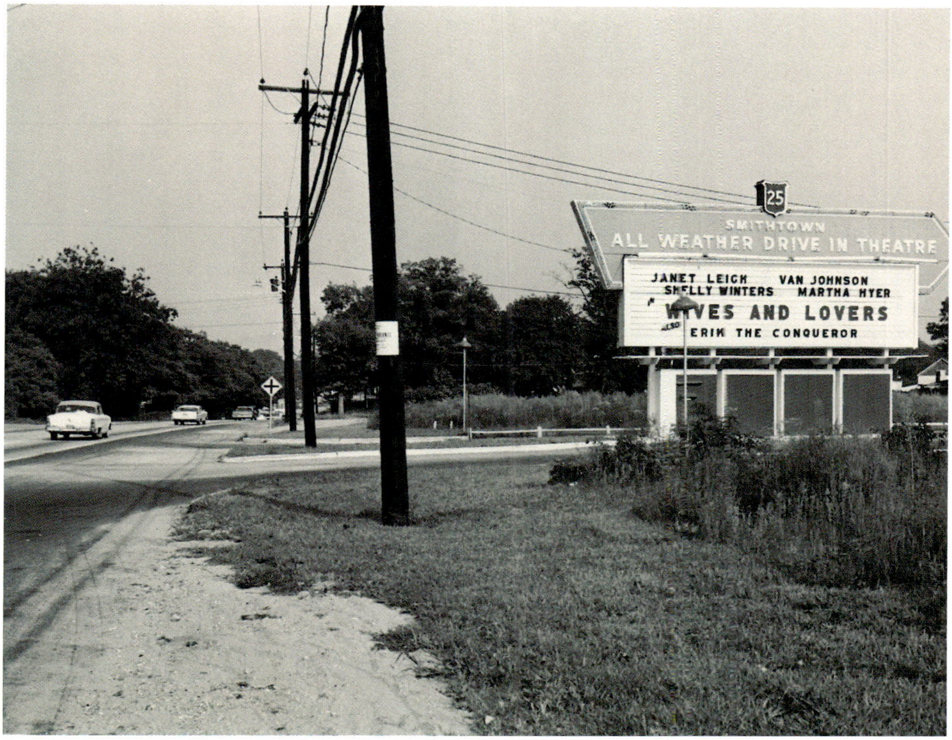

The Smithtown All Weather Drive-In Theater was located in Nesconset just east of Route 347 with an entrance on the south side of Middle Country Road, where the Country Pointe condominiums are located today. It was an all-weather drive-in, because it had an indoor movie theater attached to the refreshment stand. Opened in the 1950s, the theater remained a popular place to see movies into the 1970s, when multiplex theaters began to attract customers away from the quainter drive-ins.

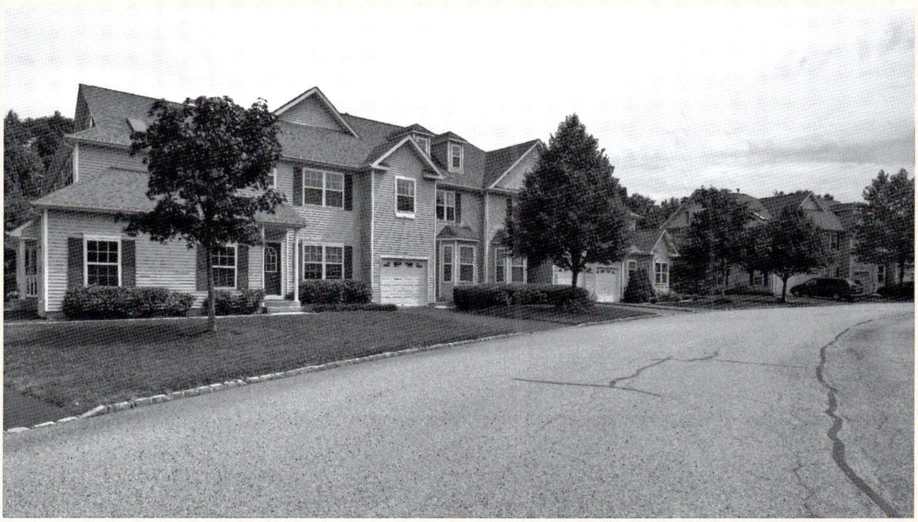

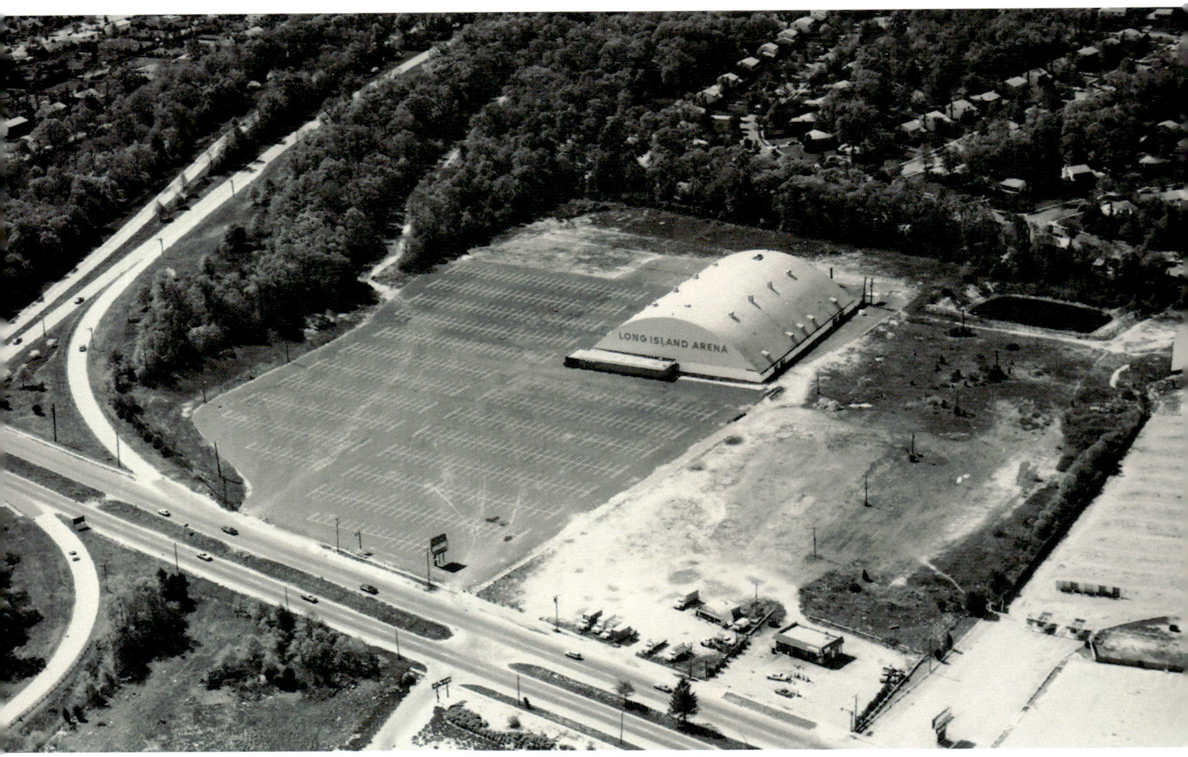

Opening its doors in 1959, the Long Island Arena in Commack was the site of a great variety of entertainment for all age groups. The indoor venue thrived through the 1960s and 1970s, when it played host to home games of the Long Island Ducks hockey team, concerts by rock bands Blue Öyster Cult and Black Sabbath, and rallies for presidential candidates Richard Nixon and John Kennedy. Today, a huge shopping complex of box stores has replaced the arena. (Historic photograph courtesy Smithtown Planning Department.)

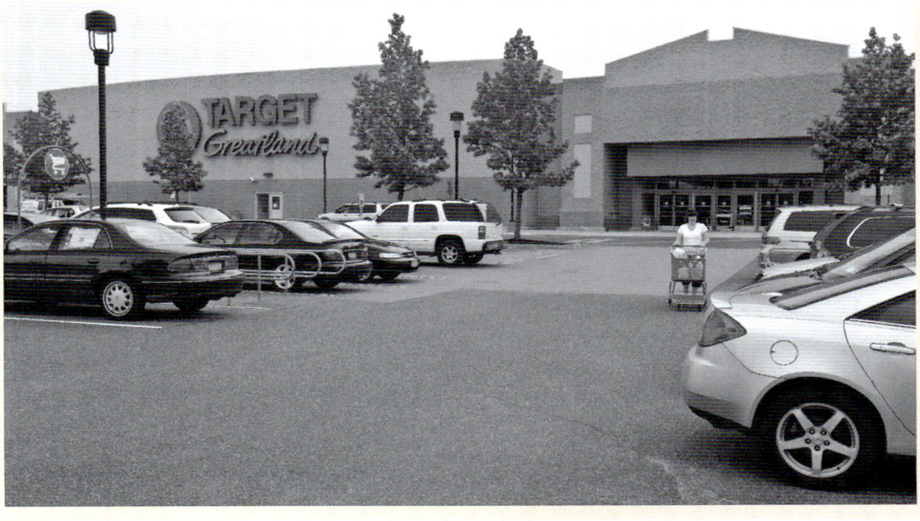

CHAPTER 5

DOWN ON MAIN STREET

CHANGING STREETSCAPES

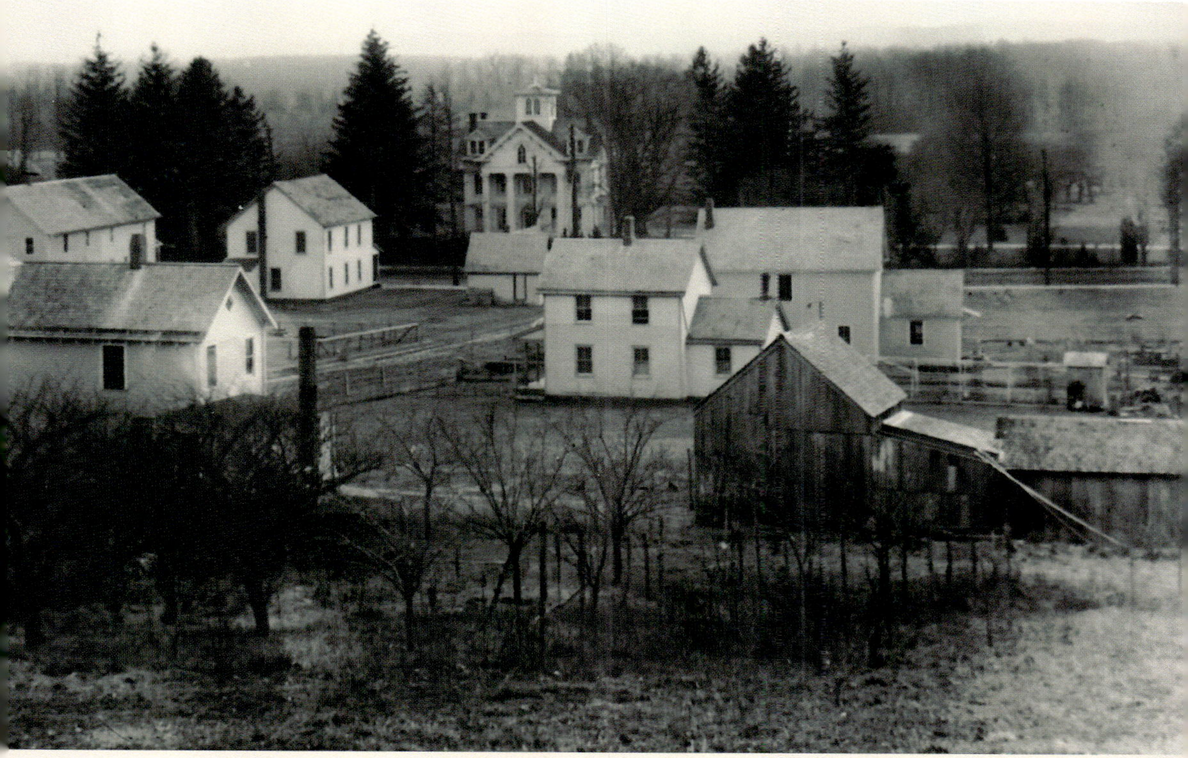

This view of Smithtown Branch from Golden Hill provides a glimpse of the country village around 1910. The Miller House dominated the south side of Main Street. The Smithtown Branch Post Office stood on the north side of Main Street, opposite the Miller House. To the left of the post office was Royal Arcanum Hall and beyond that was Huntting's General Store.

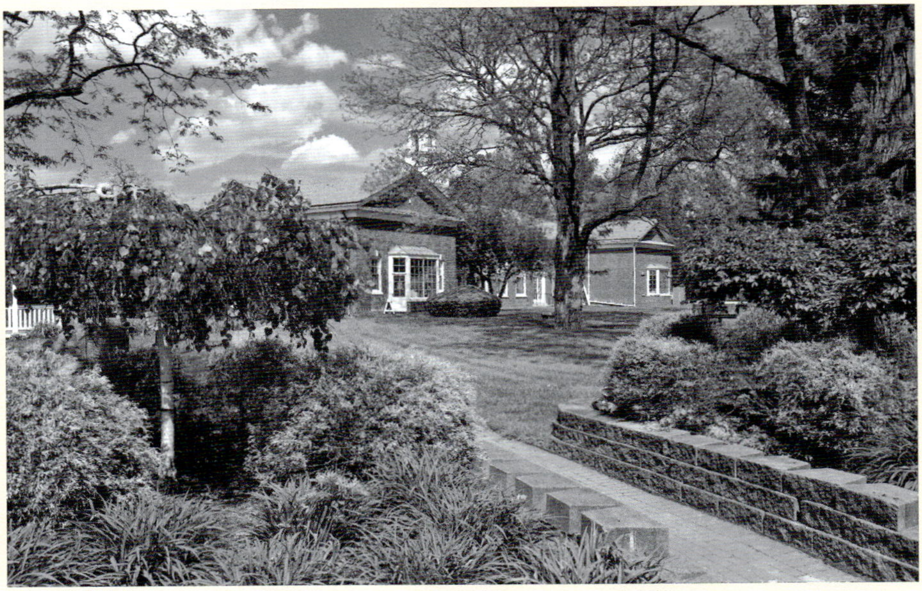

Residents will easily recognize the familiar 1912 brick structure that still exists and is now the east facade of the larger town library's main branch. However, the old photograph shows it at a different location: across the street from the Village Green on a half-acre property roughly in the center of what is now Route 111. It was moved to its present location and enlarged in 1952.

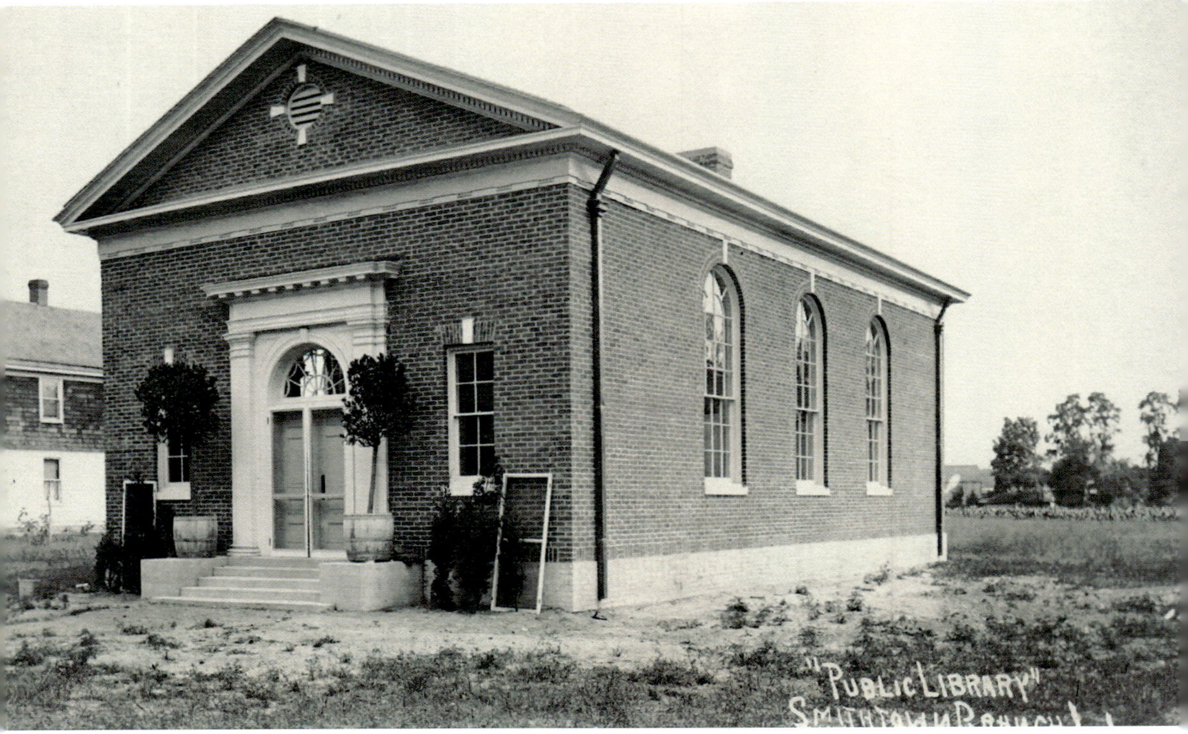

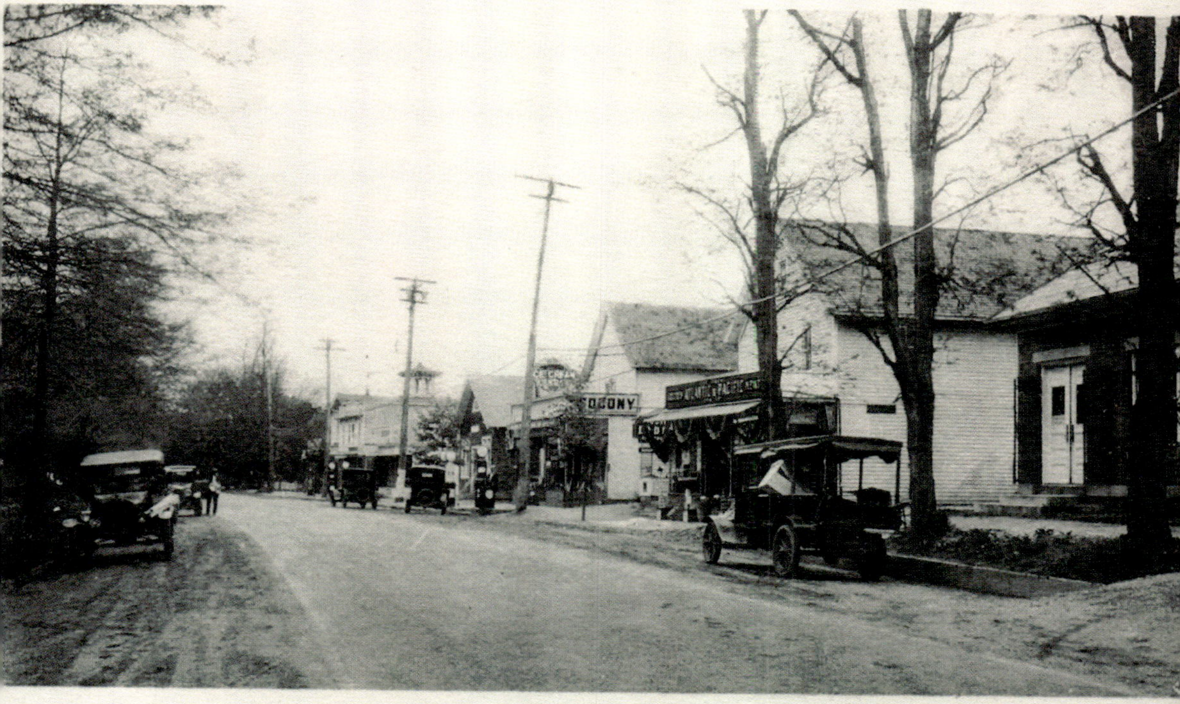

MAIN STREET, SMITHTOWN BRANCH, LONG ISLAND, N. Y.

Though now obscured by a tangle of wires and traffic lights, the twin peaks of the former A&P grocery store and Freelan Jones Stationery Shop are still visible rising above Main Street. Initially constructed as two separate establishments (as seen in the postcard included here), the buildings have since been combined into a single structure. Following a renovation in the early 2000s, the structure reopened as a recording studio, insurance office, and physical therapy center.

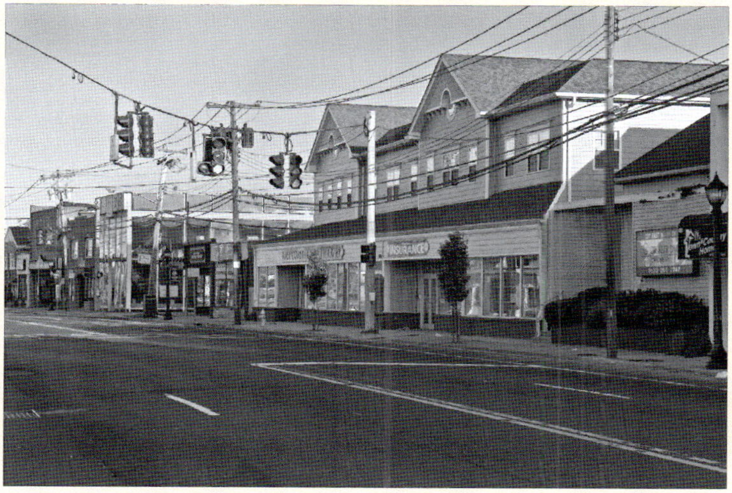

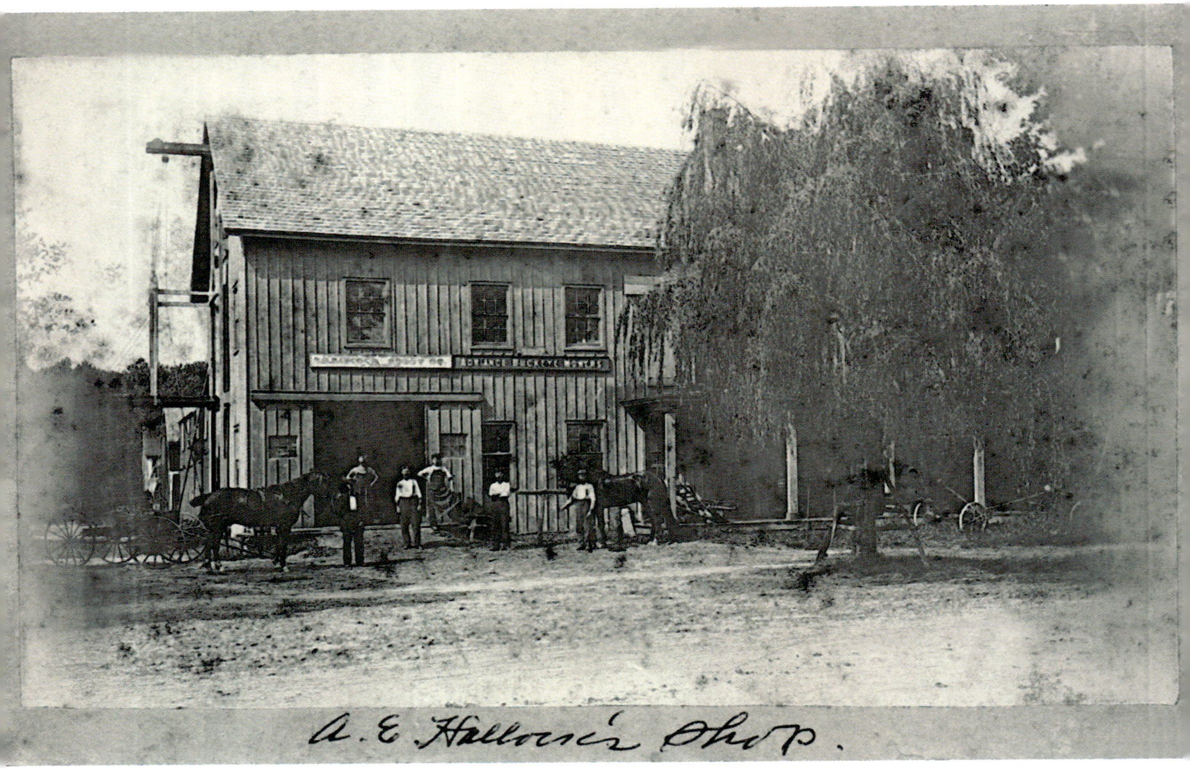

The A.E. Hallock Blacksmith Shop occupied the northeast corner of Landing Avenue and Main Street until the huge three-story structure burned to the ground in 1908. The only building on the site to survive the blaze was the Hallock House, which in the years following World War II was moved up Landing Avenue and placed near the railroad tracks. Lynn Nichols's Shell gas station stood on the former blacksmith shop site until the present building with multiple tenants replaced it.

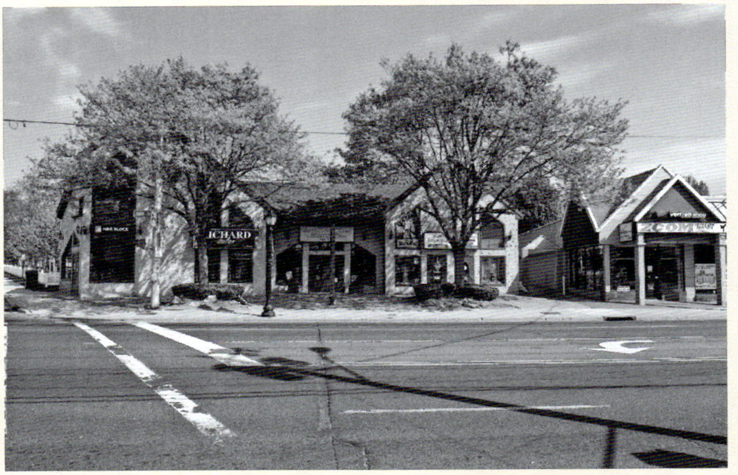

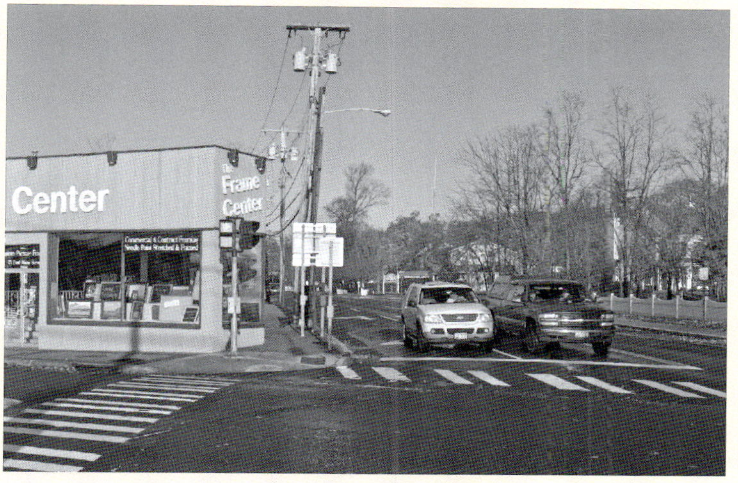

The frenetic corner at 73 Main Street, bordering Landing Avenue and now home to the Frame Center, was the location of the Landing Avenue Pharmacy, seen in the older postcard view. The contrast illustrates the town's extensive road-widening efforts in the mid-20th century. In 1940, the Landing Avenue Pharmacy was run by Anthony Naugles, a licensed pharmacist who also catered to Smithtown's sweet-toothed residents. (Historic photograph courtesy Smithtown Library, Maggie Land Blanck Collection.)

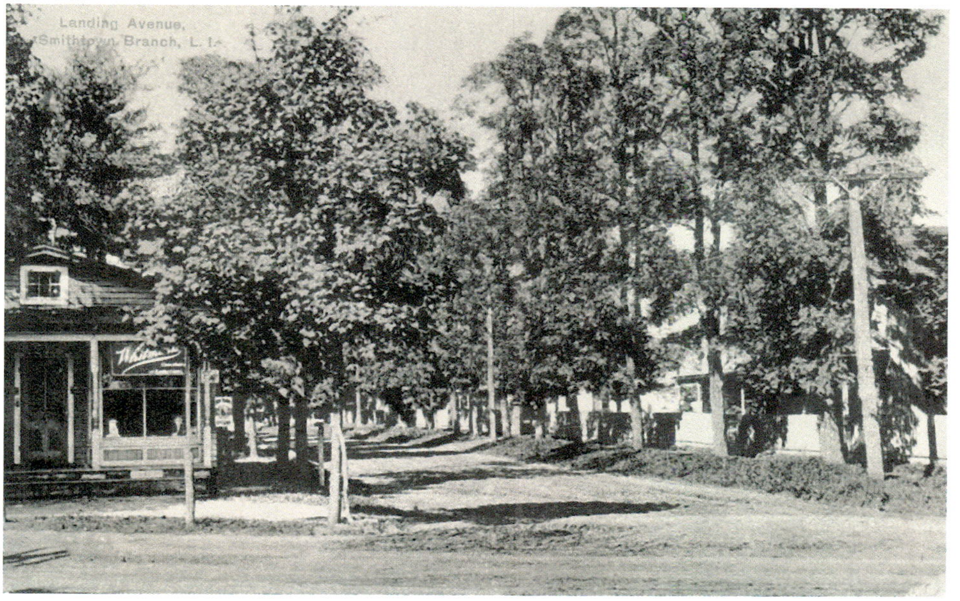

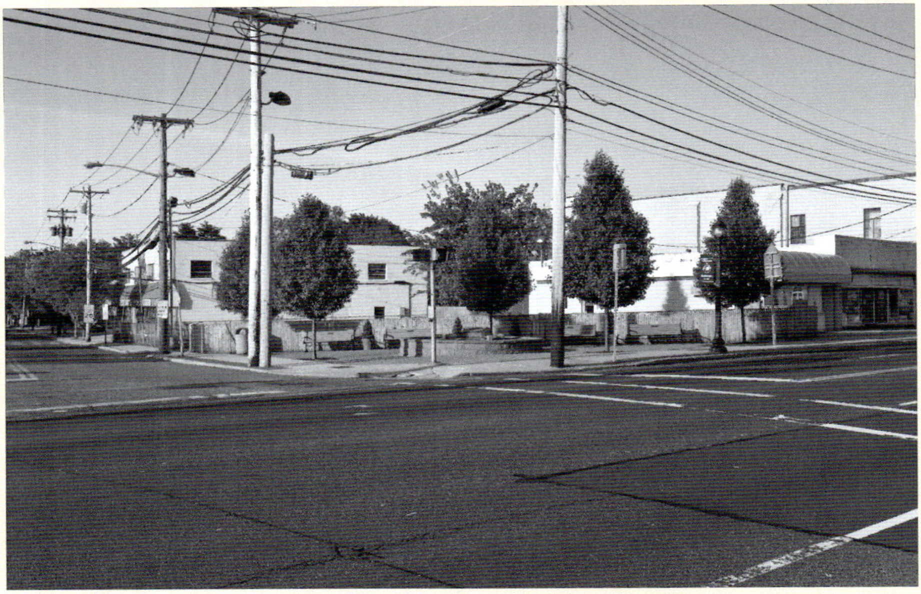

By the beginning of the 20th century, the former home of Elijah Brush had been converted into the Central Hotel, seen here around 1910. By 1928, however, the expansive building sitting on the southwest corner of Main Street and Lawrence Avenue had been torn down to accommodate the construction of the Smithtown Theater. From the 1940s until the early 2000s, the lot situated behind the current corner park played home to a series of used automobile dealerships.

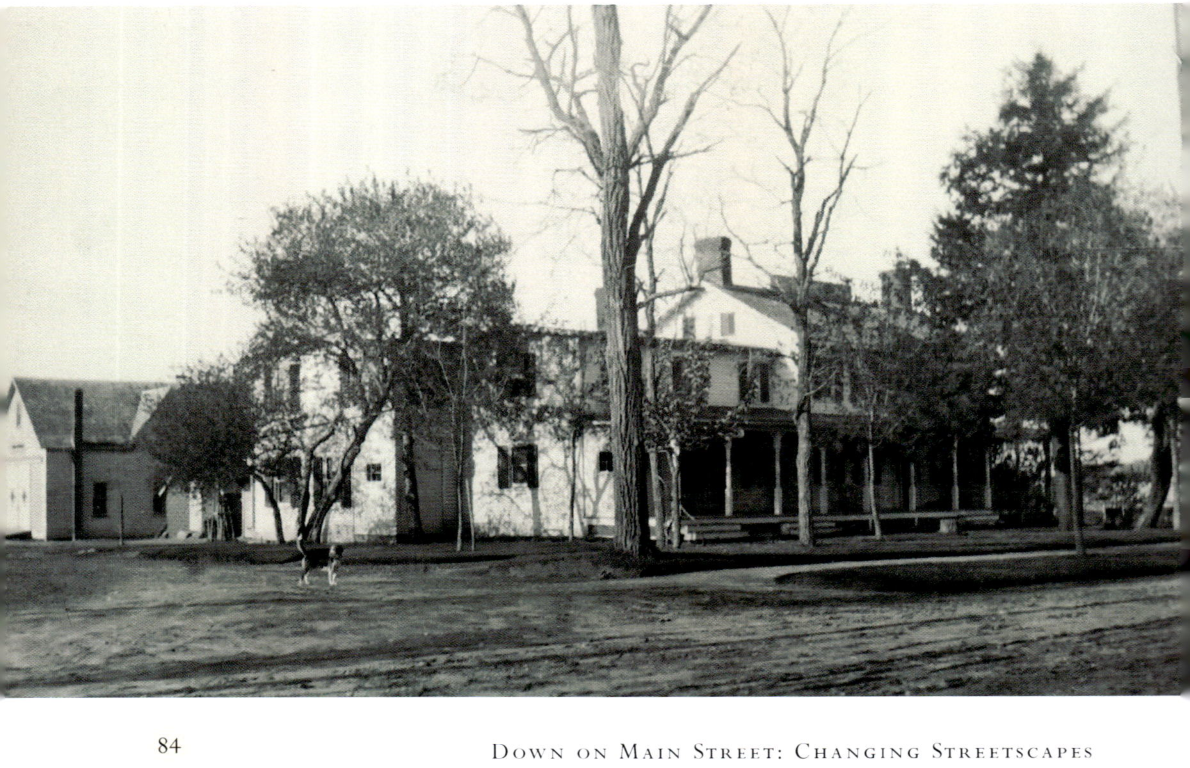

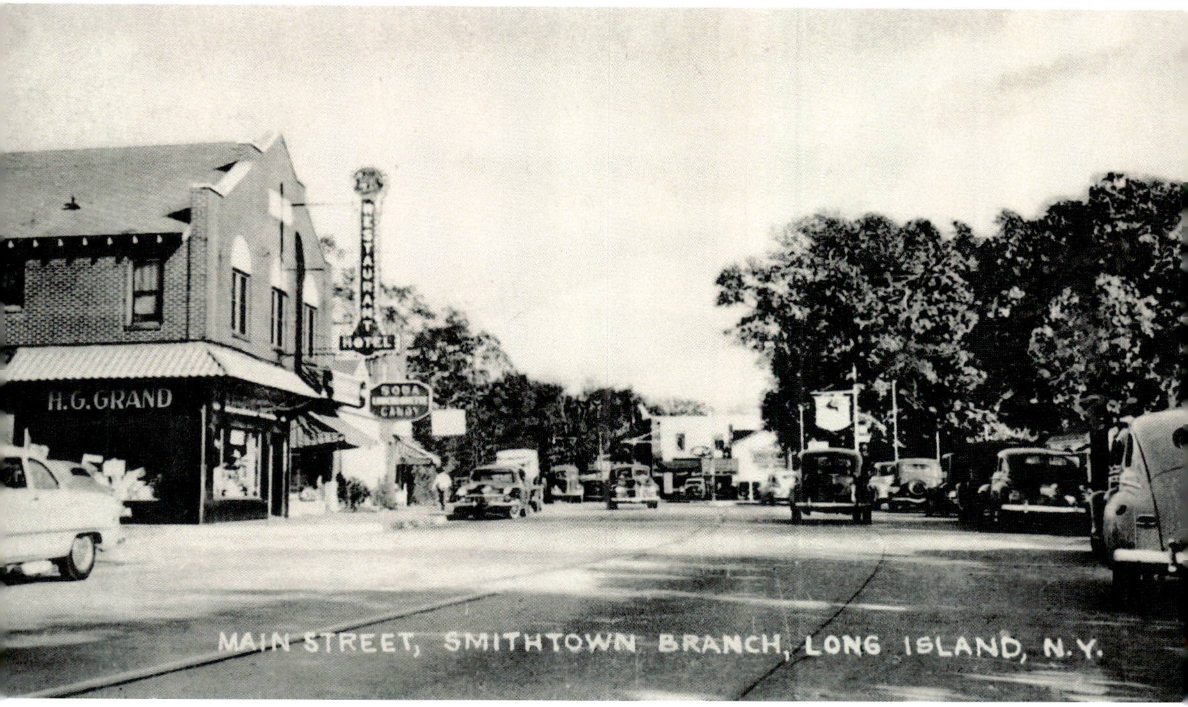

The Elks Hotel, seen here in the late 1940s, stood on the corner of Karl Avenue and Main Street, with the H.G. Grand Five and Dime and George Dounias's Sweet Shop as tenants. Beyond the Elks Hotel was Joe Land's Traffic Coffee Shop. Further east, the facade and marquee of the Smithtown Movie Theater and the Glamore Ford Agency are visible on the south side of Main Street. This part of Main Street looks much as it did 60 years ago.

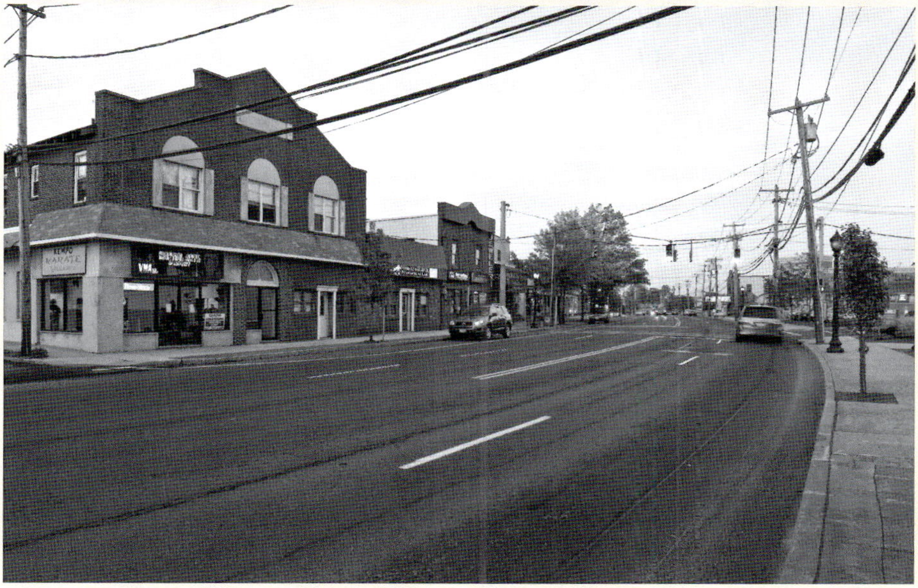

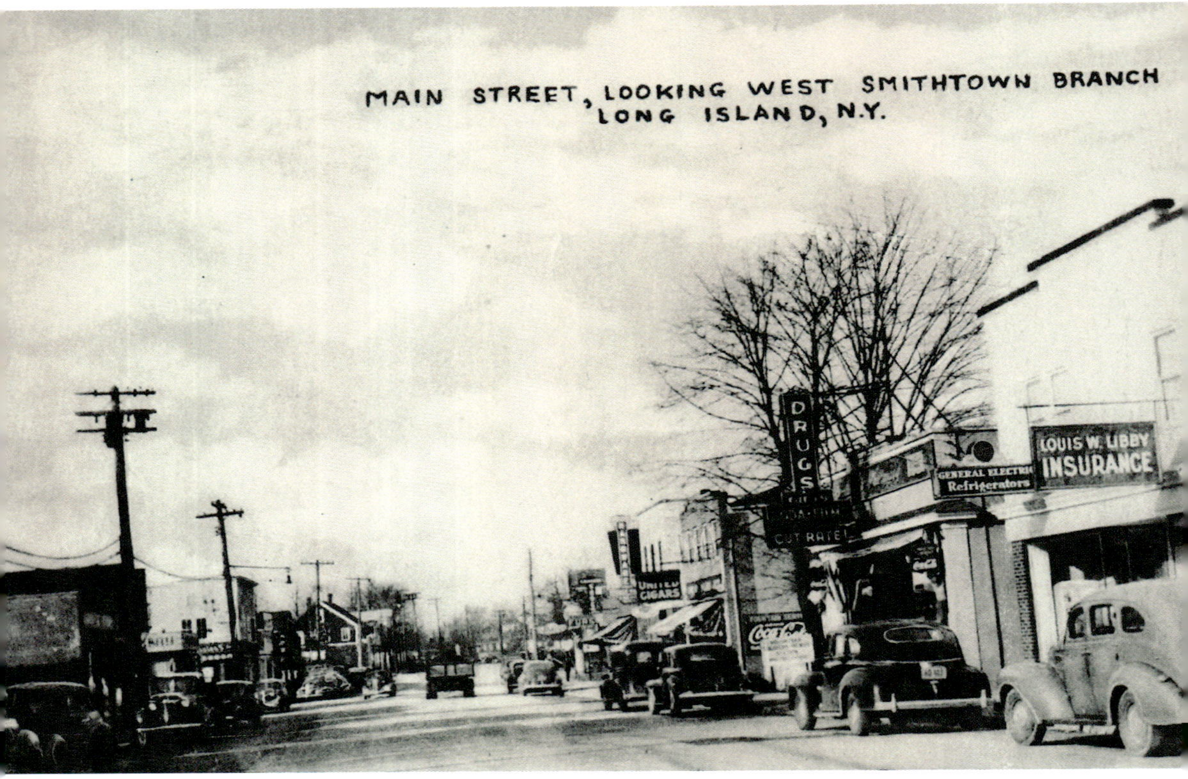

This late-1940s view of Main Street in Smithtown Branch looking west from Karl Avenue shows what the area looked like 60 years ago. During the 1940s, the stores on the north side of Main Street included Louis Libby's Insurance office, Macheck's General Electric Appliance Store, Kaplan's drugstore, Kass's Stationery Store, Alex Cohen's Hardware Store, Gouras's Fur Shop, Giacona's Shoe Repair Shop, and Shubert's gas station.

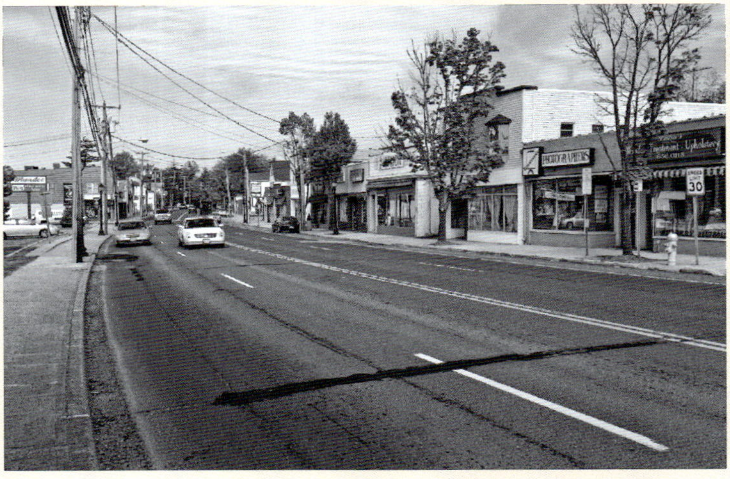

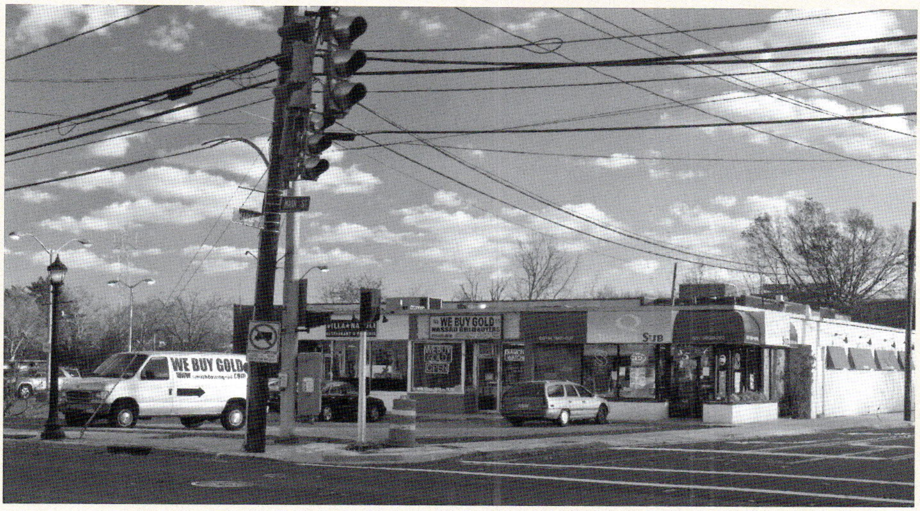

The Smithtown Bakery and Frank Radau's Blue Jay Market occupied the block on the south side of Main Street to the east of Maple Avenue when this photograph was taken in 1962. By then, the Smithtown Bakery was a landmark known for its delicious German baked goods and pastries. Frank Radau had the first supermarket in town where customers did their own shopping and brought their items to a checkout counter, where the clerk tallied items on a cash register.

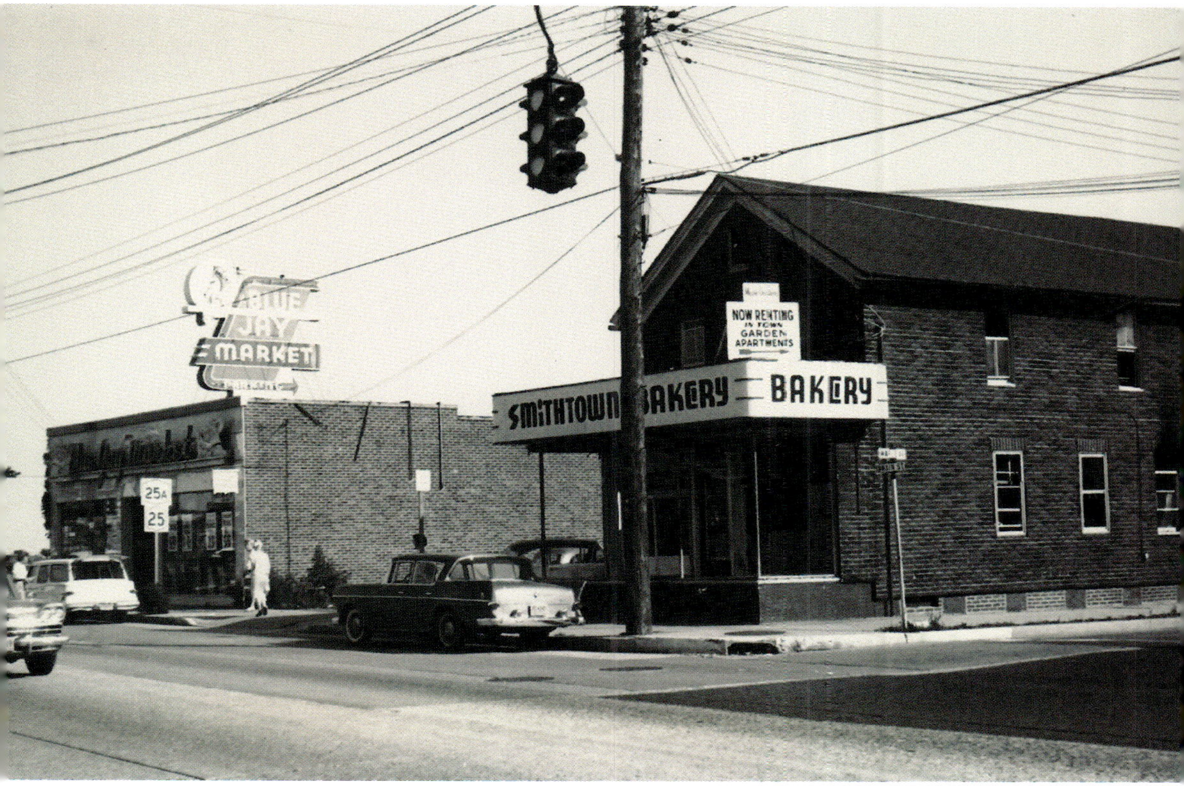

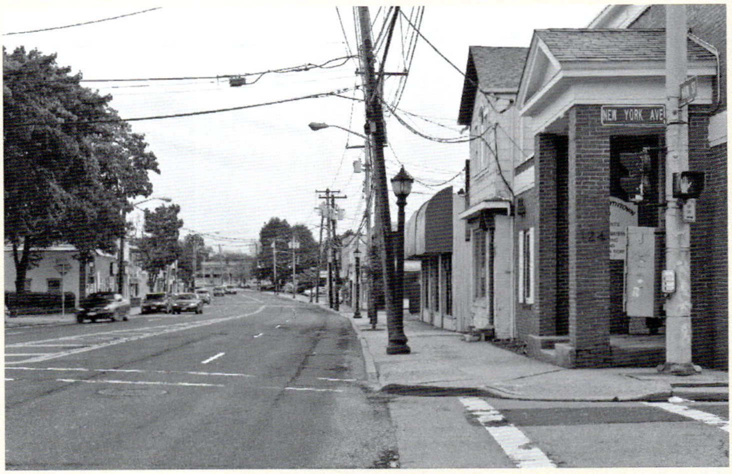

Though the block extending east from the southeast corner of New York Avenue and Main Street has a more cluttered feel today, the character of the area has changed relatively little over the past 80 years, as is demonstrated by postcard seen here. During the 1920s, this section of Main Street hosted Harnisch's Butcher Shop (the gable-roofed building at right) and Brown's Hardware Store (the building with the "Paint" sign hanging in front), among other businesses.

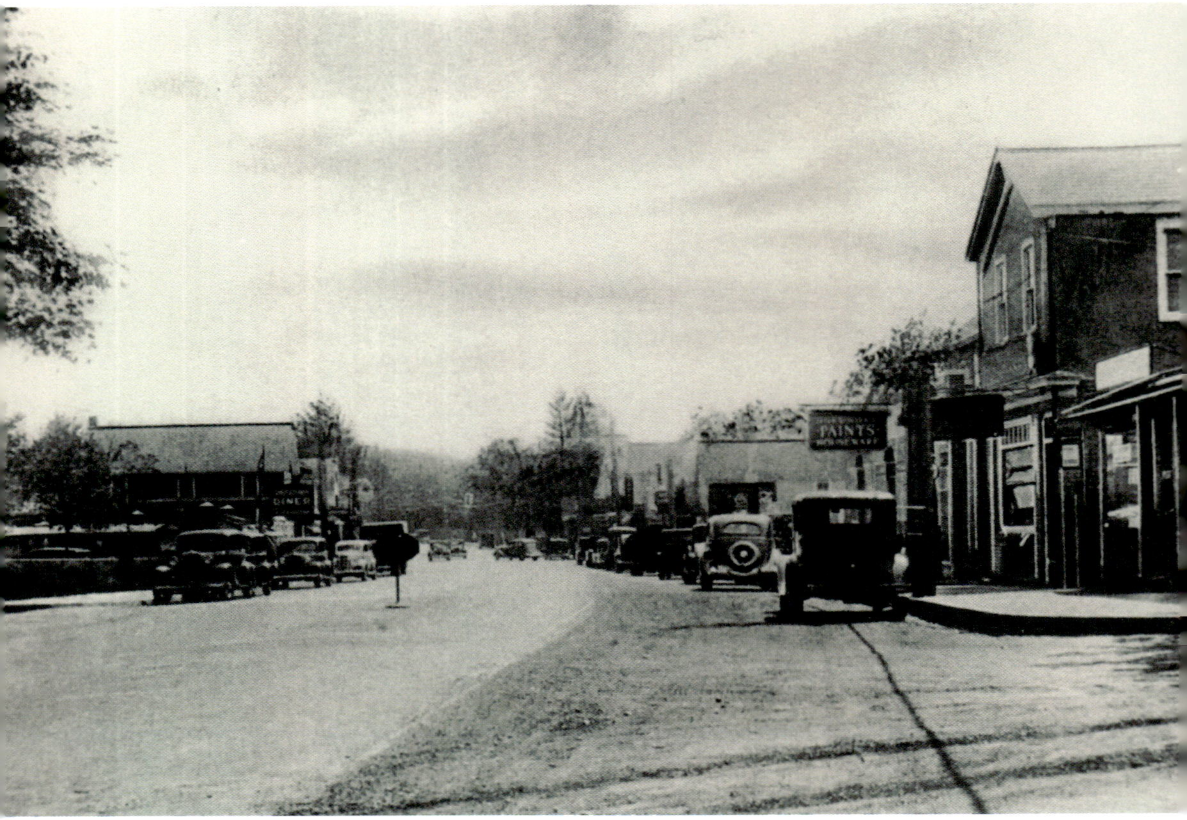

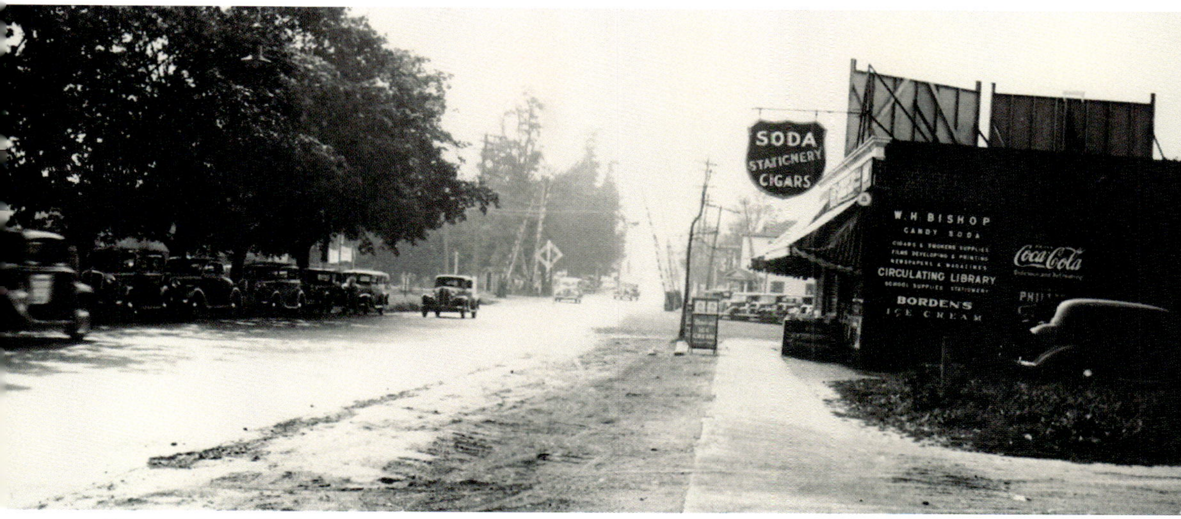

A number of storefronts in Smithtown have maintained their original contours and footprints. The business in the historic photograph marked "Soda/Stationary/Cigars" was run by William Bishop. In addition to the wares advertised in the sign, it carried fishing supplies, candies, typewriters, and newspapers. Bishop was also director of the Bank of Smithtown, and a newspaper columnist observed that he was rarely behind the shop's counter "he is not much on the show, but a great deal on the go."

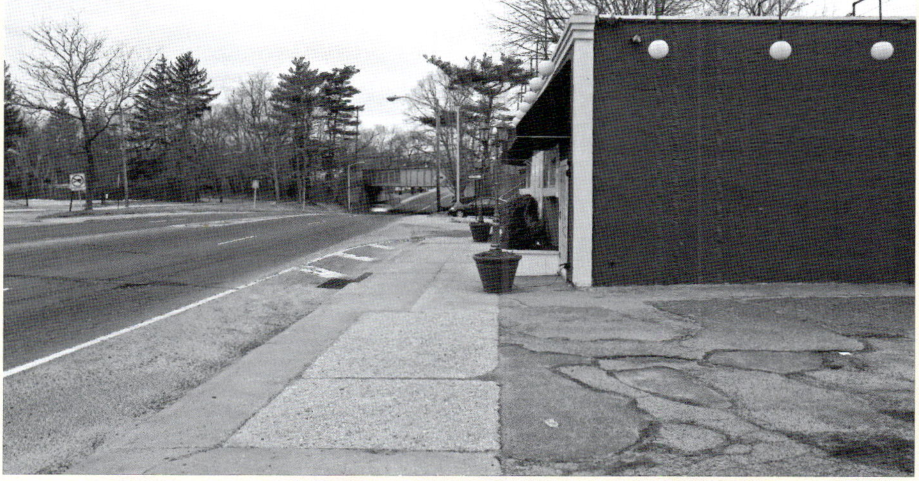

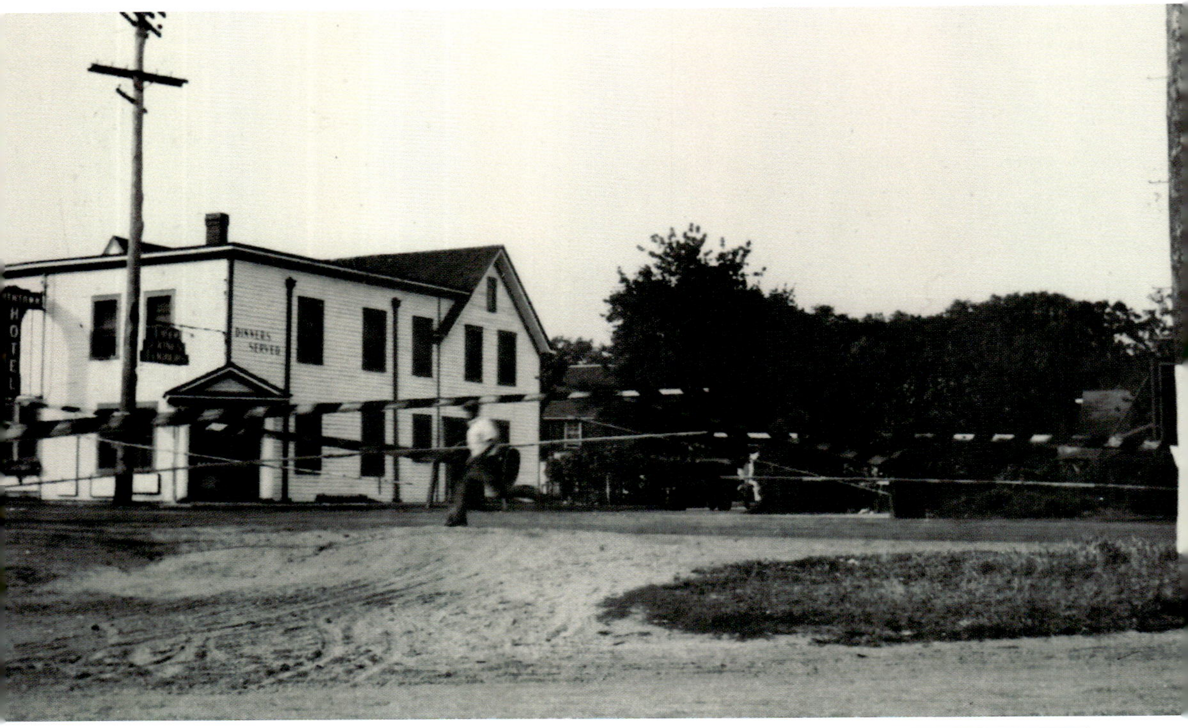

One hopes the pedestrian seen here dashing across the tracks was able to successfully evade the approaching train. Prior to the construction of the underpass in 1937, trains passing through Smithtown Branch would cross Main Street at street level. Whenever a train chugged its way through town, the crossing gates had to be hand-cranked down, and traffic came to a standstill. Allowing trains to pass above the stream of motorists, the underpass ended the tie-ups caused by the previous crossing.

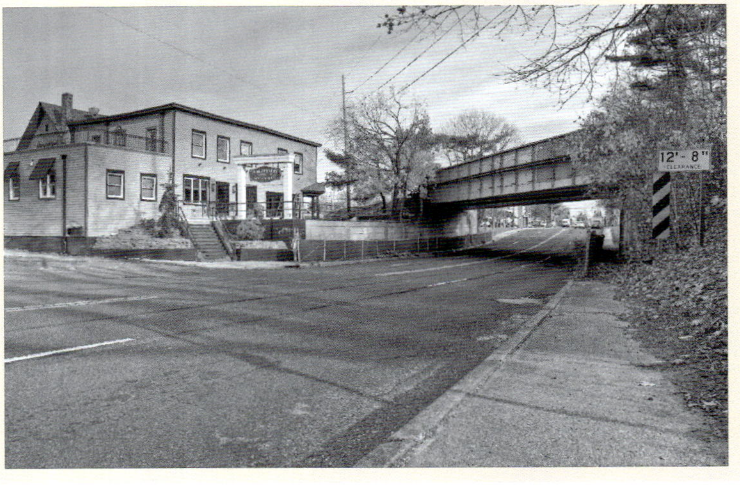

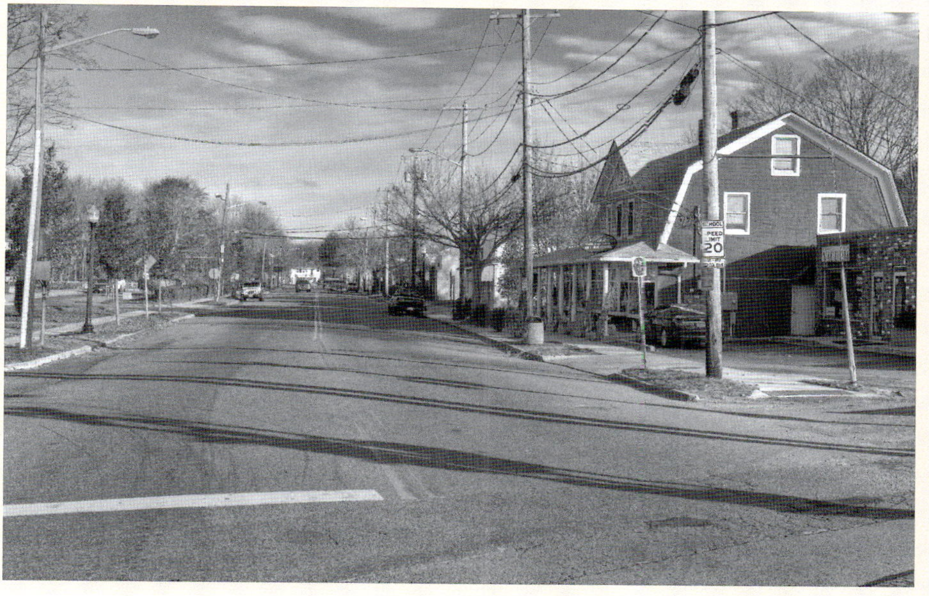

A 1941 winter storm in St. James coated the entire landscape with ice. This view of Lake Avenue, looking north from the railroad tracks, shows the building that once housed Pop Noftsinger's Hardware Store. For years, St. James residents shopped at this store, which carried every conceivable hardware item available. The St. James Post Office was located in this building during World War II, and Mitzi Duetzman remembered people gathering there anxiously awaiting letters from those in the service.

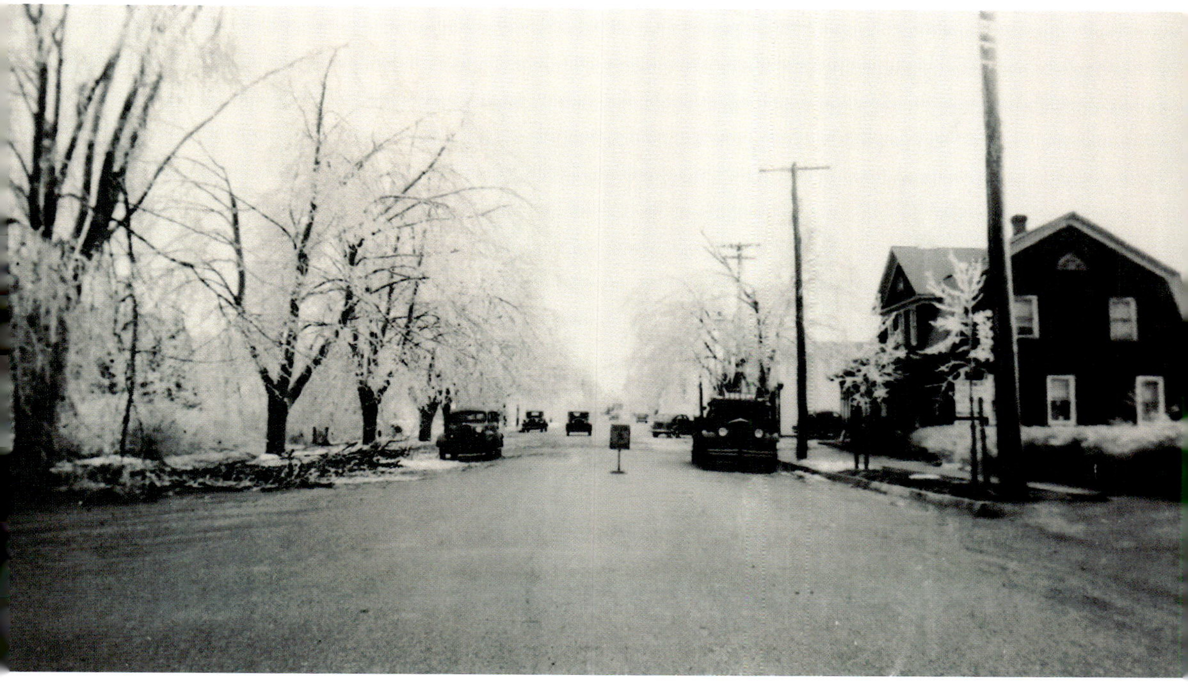

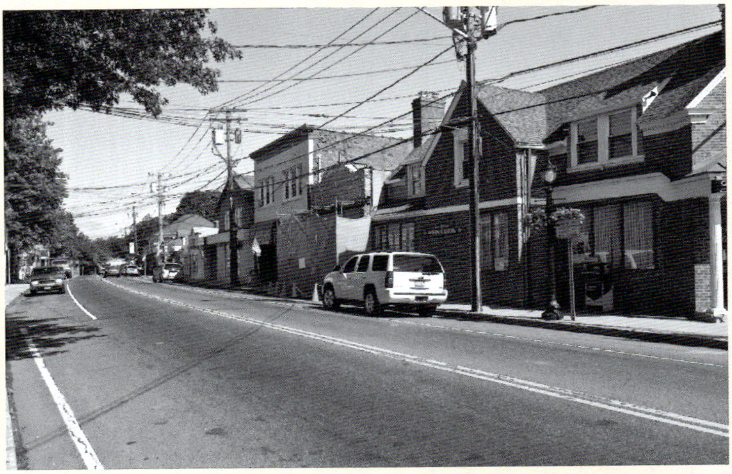

With awnings and visible signs projecting over the sidewalks, this section of Broadway (now Main Street) in Kings Park, seen here around 1936, was more pedestrian friendly than it is today. Curbside parking on both sides of the street made the stores accessible to patrons. Although 80 years have passed since this photograph of Broadway was taken, today's streetscape still looks much the same. Even the variety of retail stores of the past is found along this strip today.

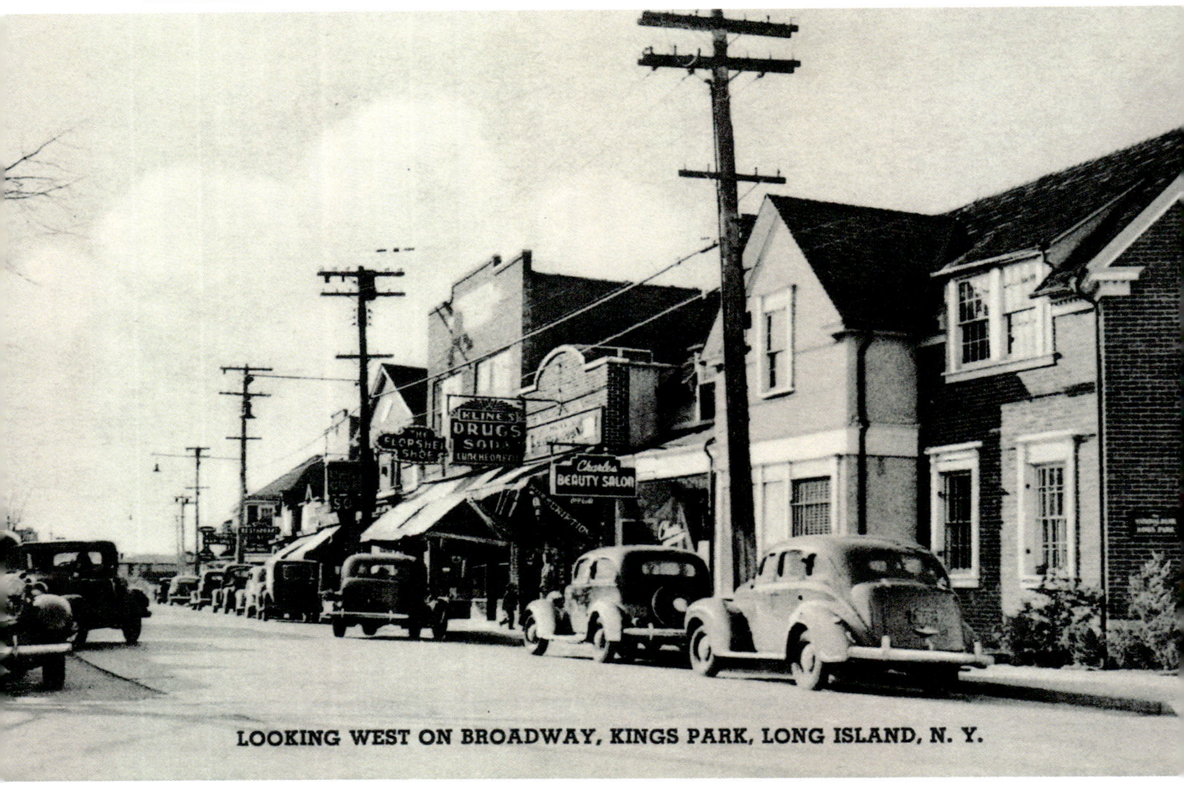

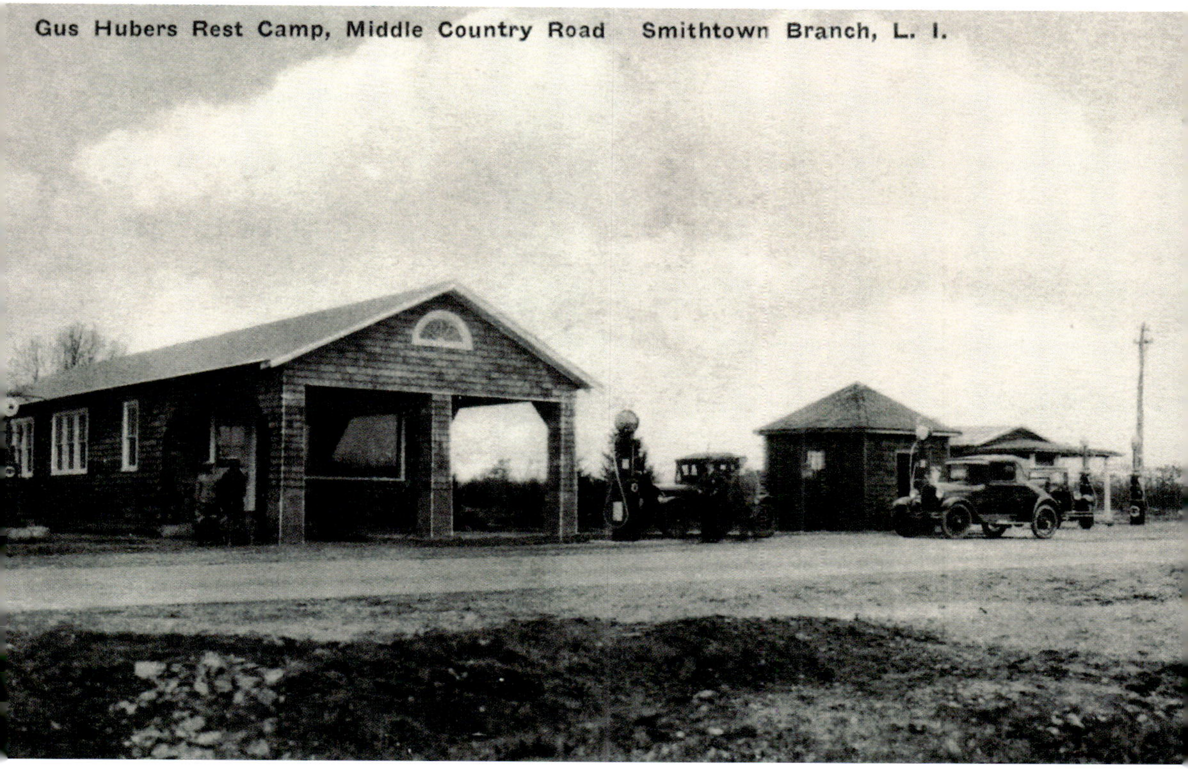

Traveling east along Route 25 today, drivers pass a throng of auto-related businesses. The automotive fixation was also true nearly 80 years ago, when Gus Huber's Rest Camp provided a full service station and rest stop at this site. Other service stations nearby included Esso, Texaco, and Dorfer's Tydol Gas Station, where, according to one chronicler, "you get the best of gas and oil supplies and a good friendly talk to boot."

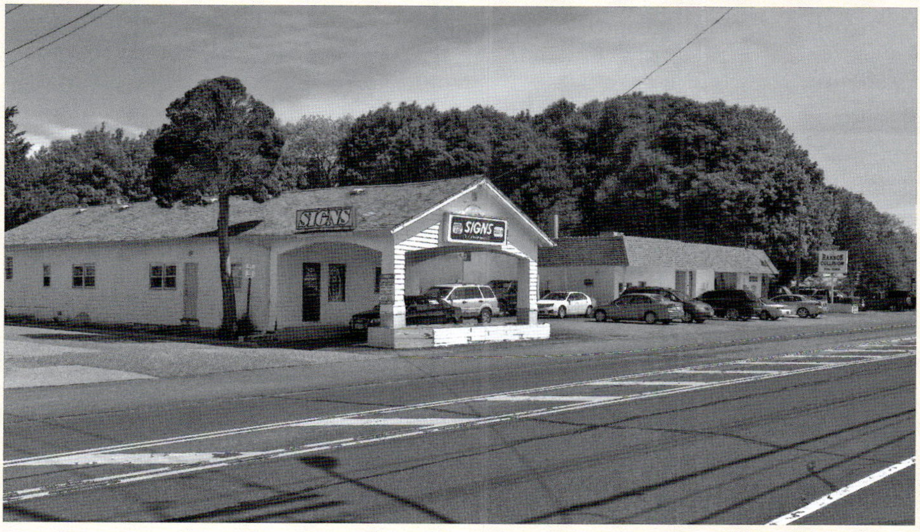

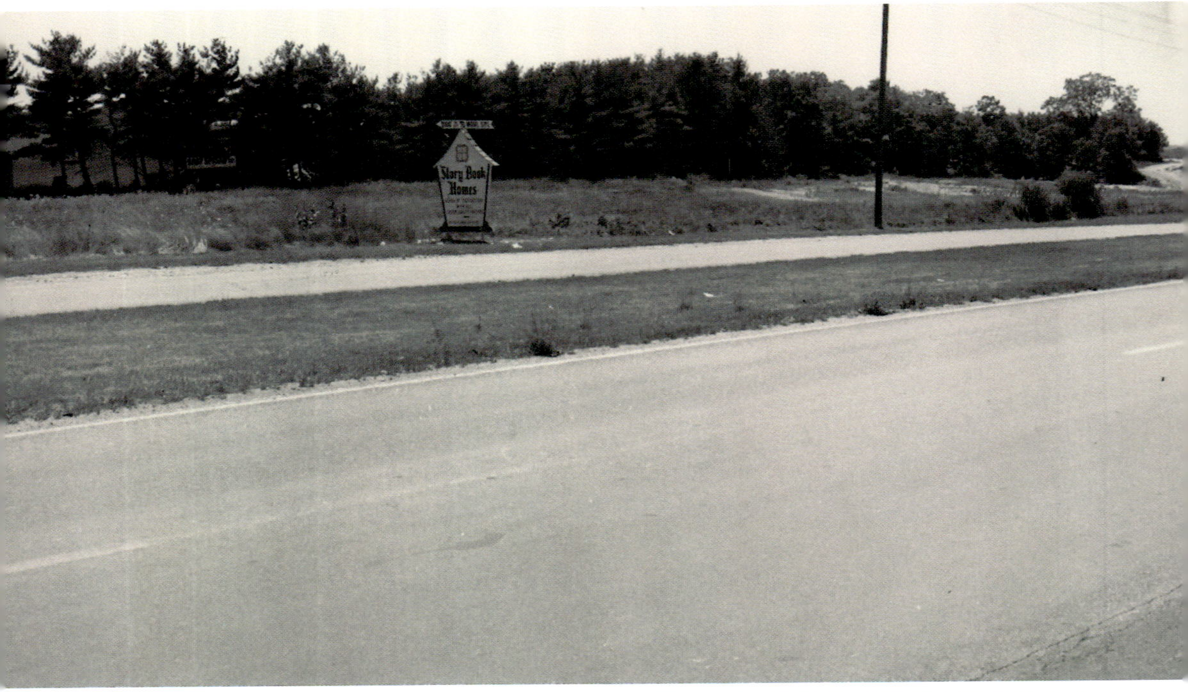

Constructed in 1955, Nesconset Highway was designed to create a quicker route for motorists traveling through Smithtown. For the first decade it was open, this stretch of road was rather quiet, flanked, as seen in the 1966 photograph, by the open fields and farms that decorated Nesconset's landscape. By the 1980s, however, the pastoral environment had given way to a string of shops and businesses; the once-sleepy roadway had become a bustling hub of commerce and traffic jams.

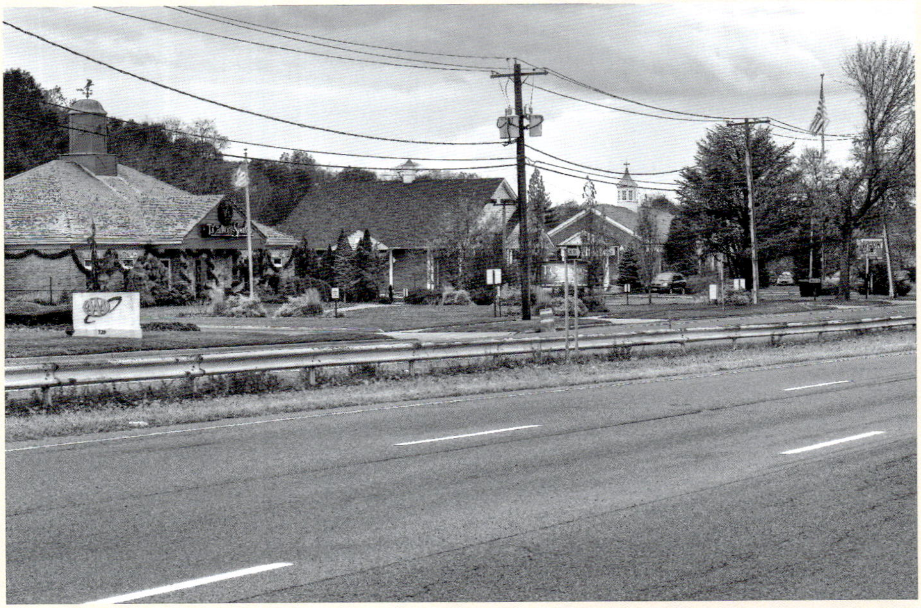

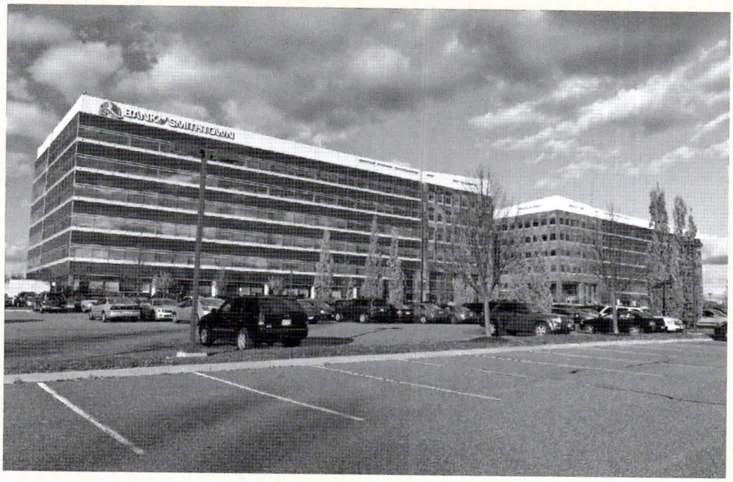

During the 1940s, International Telephone and Telegraph (ITT) operated its telephone antenna farm—a venture that facilitated long-range communications during and after World War II—on the vast acreage of what would become the Hauppauge Industrial Park. As ITT began selling its property in the 1960s, plans created by county planning director Lee Koppelman and implemented by Smithtown supervisor John Klein guided the development of the massive business center. Today, the industrial park provides employment to over 50,000 Long Islanders.

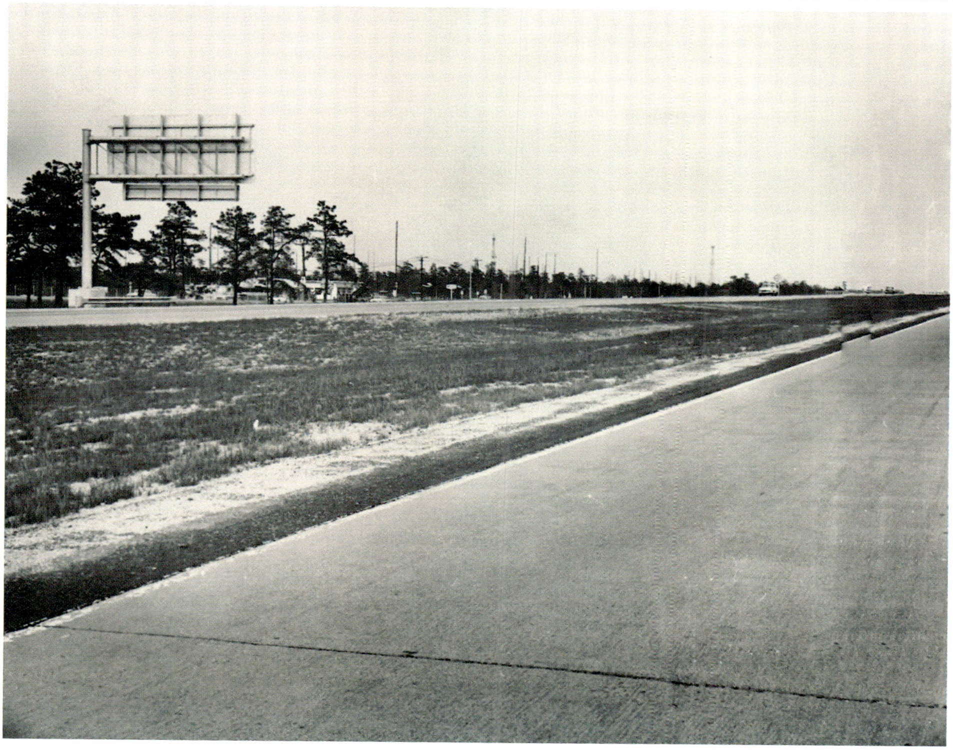